The Kingdom
in Motion

By
Bishop Tudor Bismark

Published by Truebrand Publishing
820 S. MacArthur Blvd., Ste 105-301
Coppell, TX 75019
www.truebrandmarketing.com

All Scripture quotations are from the King James Version of the Bible.

Content Development: Gary Wilde, M.Div.

ISBN   0-9725533-0-4
Printed in the United States of America

I wish to dedicate this book to my wife, ChiChi, who is my life partner and my best friend, to my four wonderful boys, Drene, Jason, Tudor, Jr., and Bernie, and to the many Pastors and ministers on the African continent who are pouring out their lives for the sake of the Kingdom!

CONTENTS

The Kingdom in Motion—Right Where You Are

When Jesus walked upon this earth, multitudes heard Him speak. They all saw Him; they all heard what He said. But Jesus said to His closest twelve followers, "They don't see, even though their eyes are open. And they don't hear, even though they're not deaf. But you are blessed because you see and you hear."

Are you one of those blessed ones, too? You are if you're willing to see and hear everything the Lord seeks to convey into your life. For it is possible to be in the Kingdom of God and have eyes and ears that God has opened to His freshness, His new and creative ways in the world today. With eyes that God has opened, you will see things that others still aren't seeing. You will be moving with the Kingdom in Motion.

My hope is that you will begin to see what the Kingdom is doing, right where you are. Where I am, in Zimbabwe, for instance, much is happening, even though I see people leaving and going all over the world to make their living elsewhere. I wonder why they are departing, when the blessing of God can be right here where we are. It just depends on the way we see—do we see all the opportunities of service God has placed before us?

How do you look at what God is doing in your personal life and in your community? Please know that, through this book, and in myriad other ways, Jesus is addressing you, as well, when He said to a few of His close followers long ago: "I am teaching you something that is coming in the future. The Holy Ghost is going to be poured out upon a coming generation. He will reveal all truth."

See What God Is Doing Today

The Kingdom of God is being manifest in awesome ways today, all across the world. I was flying home from Amsterdam recently, and a certain friend of mine, Andrew Wutaunashe, sat beside me. He had started an international organization called Family of God and had just come from a series of meetings he'd conducted in the former Soviet Union. It was a revival of unprecedented quality in that part of Asia Minor. He told me that on the first night he arrived, he was completely exhausted from his flight and that he just wanted to go to bed. So, early the next morning, since he was the Keynote Speaker at the crusade, he told everyone he was just going to say a few words. But when he opened his mouth and raised his hand, the power of God came in and placed crowds of people before him.

From that point on, he never saw so many raw miracles in his life—healings of all manner of sickness and distress. He spent four days there preaching the Kingdom of God with a tremendous manifestation of divine power, because he went in the name of the Kingdom, not to build his own organization.

The point is: What God is doing today goes far beyond the scope of just a single church with four walls. No, he is bringing whole regions, and whole countries under the influence of the Kingdom. Let me illustrate with three brief examples . . .

• **Argentina.** Forty years ago, this country was 99% traditional Catholic. But today, 60% of its current population is powerfully filled with the Holy Spirit; people are now living according to the biblical standard of "the just shall live by faith." How can a nation go from almost everybody being steeped in a seemingly lifeless and formal traditionalism to knowing the power of the blood of Jesus Christ? It is God's Kingdom in motion. So many Argentine believers are now serving the Lord faithfully and growing closer to Him through Kingdom living!

• **Colombia.** Similar things are transpiring in Colombia. In cities like Bogota and Cali, we're seeing the church rise up powerfully where lifeless churches used to be. In the past, to have five hundred members meant a big church. Today, in Cali, the average-sized church has ten-, twenty-, even forty-thousand members! Did these things happen overnight? No. They happened through the deliberate planning of men and women who came together in dedicated leadership. They chose to put their differences aside and believed that God was able to do awesome things.

• **Zimbabwe.** A number of remarkable things are happening in my own home country. Soon we'll be moving away from the situation of the average church, in which two or three thousand worshipers gather on Sunday. We're about to start breaking the ten-thousand barrier as a norm. Within the next five years there will be some churches in the city of Harare having twenty-five thousand members in attendance. What a massive outpouring of God's Spirit!

Why are these things happening? First and foremost, it's because these are places where key apostolic leaders have realized that they must put their differences aside. They recognized each other's giftings. And when they did that, they witnessed an anointing come upon their local church. And that anointing began to influence an entire nation.

Secondly, pastors in significant positions are realizing that they really do need each other. In seeking to minister to one another, they're praying Kingdom prayers together—especially that God will protect them and their people as they seek to serve him with whole-hearted commitment. God is answering.

Thirdly, these things are happening because we have a new blossoming of childlike faith. It is because of the simple faith to believe that we're now seeing the possibilities of the Kingdom. Such belief flows from a renewed passion to know God and experience His Kingdom blessings.

It's My Passion: The Kingdom

What does this have to do with your life in specific, practical terms? Consider this: when you live in the Kingdom, you live as a whole person. Salvation brings wholeness into every area of your life. You find that you are able to live at peace with your family members. You begin to experience joy and satisfaction in your work and in your ministry in the church. You can love across all barriers of race, economics, or culture. You find that the love of Christ infuses your heart to the point that it simply must flow out to others in works of humble service.

What kind of life could be any fuller than this? The Kingdom message builds bridges to all peoples, resolves conflicts, heals sorrows, and forgives sins. We are called to taste and see just how good the Lord is in our midst. We receive a foretaste here, awaiting the full manifestation of the Kingdom to come—our eternity with the Lord in heavenly places.

It's always been a passion of mine to understand the Kingdom and preach it wherever I go. It's a prime focus of my teachings in New Life Ministries, or Jabula—our place of ministry based in Zimbabwe. This ministry, or "household," has a treasure that we draw from; it's a well of anointing (see Isaiah 12) where we draw from the wells of salvation. We draw from this treasure box new things, but also old things which are the foundational structures of the Kingdom of God. We cannot build a new thing without having the foundation of the old. That's why we have to use the Word of God to test what we're teaching, to test where we are.

The theme of this book is something new that is based in the plan of God from of old: the Kingdom of God in Motion. It's a panoramic view of the Kingdom, highlighting a number of Scripture passages in the Gospel of Matthew. It is not an exposition of Matthew, per se. But each chapter will tell you what part of this Gospel is being considered, as a starting place for personal application. The key to benefiting from this approach is to keep asking yourself questions like these as you read:

- How is God speaking to my heart right now?
- What new insight about the Kingdom am I picking up here?
- What movements of the Kingdom do I discern in

my own life, neighborhood, city, or nation? How can I be a part of this movement?

- In what ways is God calling me to take action, to leave behind my comfortable status quo?
- How can I be salt and light in my world, today and tomorrow?
- What will it mean for me to take the first step toward a deeper commitment to Kingdom values?

You will be spurred to ask other questions of yourself, as well, as you open your heart to the ministry of the Holy Spirit. But these should help you get started.

What about You—Ready to Move?

Yes, the Kingdom is my passion. But what about you? Are you inspired to learn and grow and move with God's motion in your world?

Realize that this blossoming of the Kingdom was heralded long ago in many ways and many places. The prophet Amos writes in 9:13—"Behold, the days come, saith the LORD, that the plowman shall overtake the reaper, and the treader of grapes him that soweth seed." The prophet announces that a day of restoration is coming. God is going to build something that was built in the past; it will be a present blooming of something that has already been established. Something is going to get a life!

The thing built in the past was the tabernacle of David, which was an institution of God's Kingdom coming to the earth. Sadly, Israel failed to understand this.

You see, God wasn't merely interested in giving the Israelites a Promised Land. Rather, the more important thing was what he was going to do through them in that land. So many of them were interested in their little farm, their little inheritance; therefore, the Bible says that when they became prosperous in those things, they forgot God. When, in their riches, they should have remembered what God had done and begun to witness to the other nations around them, they failed to move. As God's people, they were supposed to be a living testimony to who the true God was and what he could do—especially how he could love and how he could graciously and generously reach out to save.

So we see, instead of a progression of the Kingdom, there was digression. And also we see a regression where the children of Israel were not growing but shrinking, all because they did not have a mindset to understand the fuller and greater purpose of God.

Let it not be the case with us today! When our Lord Jesus came, He came as a king born out of the Kingdom of David. He also came as a priest from the order of Melchizedek. He then began to set into motion a series of events that have one key purpose. That purpose was to demonstrate to us the great truth: the Kingdom of God is dwelling among you. In other words, we are about to behold (see and hear!) the glory of the Lord that's already dwelling among us.

I can say this for the same reason that I can say that the Internet was in existence in Abraham's day. We just had to grow into what we're receiving now. There are things in the heavens, in the air, that are already in existence; we just have to grow to a certain level of understanding and reception in order to be blessed by them.

Similarly, there's no doubt a new fuel is going to be discovered soon. We have been dependent on fossil fuels, but there is a fuel in existence right now that will change everything. We must grow into finding it and mining it. In addition, we are coming to a time when electricity won't be transported through wires any more. (After all, how does lightning move? It doesn't need wires.) My point is that we are moving in all ways, and in every area of endeavor on this earth. It is happening in the realm of the Spirit as well.

The Kingdom is here. It has been released among us. It is on the move, right where you are.

Will you receive it?

Will you move with it?

—*Bishop Tudor Bismark*

CHAPTER 1

First, Turn Your Thinking Around

(Based on Matthew 1—3 and 12:24-30)

Jesus knew their thoughts, and said unto them: Every kingdom divided against itself is brought to desolation; and every city or house divided against itself shall not stand.

—Matthew 12:25

When we begin reading the Gospels, it's as if we've entered an art gallery and stand transfixed before a beautiful painting. All the brilliant colors wash over us and move us. The masterful strokes of the Painter seem to thrust right into our hearts with the greatest truths the world could ever know—revelation direct from God.

In fact, each of the Gospel books is a masterwork in itself, conveying the same awesome truths but from four unique perspectives. Mark, writing to the Roman culture, focuses on the movements of Jesus from place to place. So he paints his Gospel with a certain sparseness of words as he brings us along with Jesus on the highways and byways of life.

Luke, a doctor, naturally focuses on the human condition. He fills his masterwork with people—men and women in need of healing, in need of salvation, in need of a touch from the Lord. The writing flows from his heart and touches our hearts, too, even in our modern day.

Then there is John, who constantly calls us to belief. More than any other Gospel writer, he speaks in order to persuade us. He wants us to give ourselves to the Master who is, really, the gentle Lamb of God. "You see what this Savior has done," he says. "Now believe that he did it for *you.*" With each dab of color on his splendid canvas, he calls you to take the message personally and to accept it for yourself.

Then we come to Matthew, the beautiful account of Jesus written primarily for a Jewish audience. But it is definitely for all of us, too. For it speaks of the Kingdom that is in motion and still moves forward. If Mark saw the movement of Jesus, then Matthew saw the movement of Jesus' work in the world—the new things that are coming into our world and continuing to unfold. Will we be ready to move with them? Will we merely stand before the masterpiece, or will we enter into it with heart, soul, and mind, letting the Lord carry us along for His glory?

Yes, the Gospel of Matthew speaks to the Jewish community, specifically to address the issues pertaining to them. That's why Matthew gives us several major discourses because of what the Jews believed concerning the Kingdom of God. They certainly believed there would be a restoration of the Kingdom of God, and that did happen. But it didn't happen the way they thought it would.

We find ourselves in the same plight. We know there is a restoration of the Kingdom, but it's not coming the way we've been programmed to think. Most of us who've been immersed in the Western way of thinking have assumed the Kingdom of God will be coming through a future millennium at a second return of Jesus. But it is time to think anew: *The Kingdom of God is going to be manifest here, in a very powerful way, before the catching away.* It is a theme I will come back to, time and time again, in this book.

But for now, let us look closely at this masterpiece of Jesus' words that Matthew paints for us. First we'll discern two main themes in broad brushstrokes: that Satan has an authority in the world, but that we, too, have an authority—a greater one through Jesus. Next we'll consider four great truths of the Kingdom, one at a time. These are the things Jesus was telling His disciples about the Kingdom. They are the things He wants us to know, as well.

Satan Has Authority—in the World

Let's jump right into these themes by going to Matthew 12, where we'll interrupt an unfolding series of events in verses 24 and 25. Here Jesus is responding to an accusation—that He's casting out devils by the prince of devils. But "Jesus knew their thoughts." And the first thing He points out is that *Satan has a kingdom, and that kingdom is standing.* He says, "If I, by Beelzebub, which is the prince of devils, cast out devils, by whom do your children cast them out? Therefore they shall be your judges."

He is speaking of levels of authority. After all, the "children" of these leaders, born through the concepts of religious development, do have a level of authority. Their authority can even remove devils from certain communities, societies, or individuals. They have a level "by which they function." So Jesus confronts them by saying, in effect, "They have a level by which they function, and you're saying that *My* level is under Beelzebub; then what's *their* level?"

In other words, if Jesus' level is the highest level (which it is), then obviously they have a level, right? Then He goes on to say, "But if I cast out devils by the Spirit of God, then the Kingdom of God is come upon you." The point is this: *It's possible to cast out devils not by the Spirit of God but by an authority that is invested elsewhere.* It's possible to cast out devils without the Kingdom of God being established. But if you cast out devils by the Spirit of God, then the two work together, and the Kingdom of God is thus manifest.

Then Jesus says, "Or else how can one enter into a strong man's house and spoil his goods except if he first bind the strong man, then he will spoil his house?" This is a very powerful verse. Jesus says in 12:26 that Satan has a kingdom. Now He goes from "kingdom" to "house." He says, "How are you going to spoil his house?" So there is the house of the enemy and the kingdom of the enemy.

Thus the enemy has certain authority, and he is powerful. But that is not the complete picture. There is other authority here, too—*yours!*   Amen

We Have Authority—in the House, City, Kingdom

Let's go back to verse 25: "Every kingdom divided against itself." That's the highest level, the Kingdom. "Divided against itself is brought to desolation." Then he says, "and every city." (Note: There's a grammatical feature in this particular verse in the King James Version; it's a semicolon, which emphasizes what's coming next). One translation says, "Every city (and house) divided against itself shall not stand." So here we have three levels of authority and influence: the house, the city, the kingdom. These are places for the believers' authority to shine forth.

How can you apply this personally? Consider: A lot of ministries haven't developed their house, and yet they're trying to take the Kingdom. Do you see what I mean? When the Kingdom is the third level of progression, before you can get to it, you have to have a strong house. Then you go to the city; then you go to the Kingdom. *Also, picture of the Temple 3 stages. The first steps Holy of Holies*

Look at it this way: A man cannot be a bishop of a house unless he first establishes rule and authority and order in his own home. So it starts there, then goes to the next level, then to the next level. How in the world can you get a man leading a city of leaders, of pastors, if he can't even take care of his kids? Of course, I'm not just speaking of physical children; I'm referring to spiritual sons. Sadly, a lot of spiritual children are running everywhere, and the pappy of that particular house is not taking care of them.

So . . . Think Right!

Recall that the Bible says, "He knew their thoughts and said unto them, 'Every Kingdom divided against itself is brought to desolation; and every city or house divided against itself shall not stand: And if Satan casteth out Satan, he is divided against himself; how shall then his kingdom stand?'"

With this as our launching point let's take the second broad theme in Matthew—our authority in the Kingdom—and look a little closer for the truths within it. What, exactly is the Kingdom we're given? We need to think rightly about this. I'd like to suggest four key Kingdom truths for us to know from the beginning—

Truth #1: If you're in the Kingdom, you have a life source. If we're to truly understand Jesus' reasoning in 12:25, we'll be helped by looking back to the beginning of Matthew's Gospel, in chapter 1. Matthew starts with a genealogical and chronological order concerning the coming of Jesus. It starts with Abraham, who is the father of the faith. Abraham is, here, a life source. *You cannot be a part of the Kingdom if you don't have a life source.*

The Bible says it this way: You must not crush your father or your mother, because if you crush your father or your mother, there's no longevity, and you don't have a promise of permanence. You don't have a promise of tomorrow, and your life is shortened. So Abraham is related here as a life source. He is called out of a place, sent to a land, and through the divine promise to Sarah, gives birth to Isaac. Sarah is ninety years old; Abraham is a hundred, a complete century! Here, Abraham now becomes the father, through Isaac, of many nations. And then the apostle Paul, in the New Testament, brings it right down to us: "If ye be Christ's, then are ye Abraham's seed, and heirs according to the promise" (Galatians 3:29).

The point is you and I need to remember that we are not alone in the Kingdom. We are connected, all of us, to our life source, who, ultimately, is Jesus Christ himself. Therefore we are brothers and sisters together in the Kingdom.

What, in the most practical terms, will that mean for you? Are you able to stop during the busiest part of your day and carve out a little space for recognizing God's presence with you? Are you able to hold off on an important decision in order to seek wisdom and guidance from God and from others in the Kingdom? Are you able to pull back, for a moment, from worry or rage, to remember where you are from and where you are going? All of these remembrances of the source-connection can help us learn to live with a spirit that is fed by the Spirit.

Truth #2: If you have a life source, you have a lineage. Yes, there is a lineage here. And it presents us with a number of things to understand.

First, realize that there are *gentile women locked in to the lineage of Jesus.* Look again at the first seventeen verses of Matthew and you'll see them. They are a part of the bride of Christ, or the development of the lineage of Christ. It's important for the Jewish community to understand that the Kingdom of God is broader, in terms of the bride, than just a Jewish DNA. So the many women that are put here, including Ruth, are placed within this lineage. It makes you think, doesn't it?

Second, we have shepherds that come. They had to examine the "Lamb of God" that He be a perfect sacrifice. In the lineage we have rich and poor, educated and non-educated, the powerful and the powerless. Again, the lineage is thought provoking.

Third, we have the kings, the ones who need to examine Jesus to find out whether He was truly royalty. And He was, signified by the gifts He was given. He was given myrrh, which deadens pain. He was God come to us, and the pain of being associated with the human condition had to be deadened so He could function without killing people! But at the end of his ministry, when they give Jesus myrrh to deaden the pain on the cross, then He doesn't want it. On the rough wooden instrument of torture, He freely chooses to take the pain on our behalf.

He's given frankincense, too, because His life had to be an example of true worship. Abraham said, "I'm going with my son up to the mountain, and we are going to worship." The ultimate sacrifice of taking his own son was an act of worship. So the life of Jesus was not just a sacrifice, but it was a sacrifice of praise. It was a demonstration of true worship.

Finally, Jesus was given gold. It signifies a number of things, but I suggest that the gold was given to finance the ministry ahead. Jesus was going to be employing businessmen who had a certain lifestyle and were accustomed to money flowing at any given moment. We'll see that, at the very end of the ministry of Jesus, He addressed five hundred men as He was being lifted into the heavens. These men had family but had left their children. My friend, *God is not irresponsible; He won't call you at the expense of your own children.* So Jesus was to finance this entire ministry. The money is always there; however, you've got to get to a certain place before that money unfolds.

Truth #3: If you can truly repent, you can truly enter. Now move ahead with me to Matthew 3. We find here an interruption of the ministry of Jesus, so we can know the release of John the Baptist's ministry. And John's message is overwhelmingly simple: "Repent! For the Kingdom of Heaven is at hand."

Now the word repent means to turn and face another direction. So the question addressed to your heart is:

Can you turn your thinking? Can you become totally opposed to the old way you've been thinking—because God is about to do a new thing? If you can, welcome in!

It's wonderful to realize that the people way down at the bottom in Jesus' day, the common people, were the ones who turned most readily and easily to the new thing God was doing. They hadn't been religiously programmed like their leaders. They were able to see the Kingdom in simple forms. They were able to embrace the very thing Jesus was offering them: a simple acceptance of himself, his Kingship in their lives.

On the other hand, those who were programmed with a religious mindset were looking for something else. Certainly not this Jesus as Lord. They were looking for a restoration of an old order, an old system that an old womb would birth. Therefore Jesus said to Nicodemus, in effect: "This Kingdom is so amazing that God is providing even a new womb. He's not going to give birth from an old womb; you must be born again from a new womb." This is the reason Jesus could say that John was the greatest of the prophets, the one so empowered to make the announcement that the Kingdom of Heaven is at hand.

Truth #4: If you've entered, you've opened the door. In other words, the Kingdom of God doesn't just come in, you have to open the door for it. You see, later on in Matthew 3, Jesus comes down to John and is baptized, submersed, by John. The baptizing of Jesus in the river Jordan was significant because it was a crossing over from Kaddish Barnea into the realm of promise. This is crucial for you and me: *If we're going to come into the land of promise, we have to be totally submerged—not in our own world but in the world that is preset for us.*

In other words, an older priest, who is John, had to submerge the younger priest, who is Jesus, even though Jesus had a greater rank and John recognized that. Yes, Jesus had a rank of divine "eternal priesthood" as opposed to John's rank of human "Aaronic priesthood." But *it's necessary for a man to open the door for the Kingdom.* The Kingdom doesn't come bursting in; it is your church, you as a leader, you as worshiper—you have to open the door as a human being for the Kingdom of God to come in.

What Are You Thinking Now?

Now that we've reached the end of this first chapter, I'd like to ask you: Has your thinking turned a bit? I ask because, as you study the Kingdom in Motion, you'll begin to see how important it is to be proactive. Matthew's call is more than an intellectual exercise. It is a calling from God to your heart. It is a call to action, a heavenly summons to move with the new movement of the Kingdom each day.

In fact, in Matthew 11, the Bible says that the Kingdom will be taken by force. It is a matter of actively possessing something. In this regard, I think of the promise to the children of Israel: That I, the Lord, am taking you from a land of slavery to a land of promise.

God was showing them what they would possess.

Yet that ancient people failed to fully grasp the most important thing—not the possession itself, but the reason for it. They should have opened their hearts to the greater questions: *Why* did God give us cities? *Why* did God give us houses? *Why* did God give us land? If we can understand that, then we can see the power of the Kingdom as being an infiltration into our lives that we might possess the whole world.

Therefore turn your thinking to a mindset of openness to God's Spirit, to an expectation of God's working. Join with me in this journey in Matthew, a spiritual adventure that will lead us from the negative to the positive. It will be a pathway turning us from a daily despair to boundless hopefulness, from barriers of all kinds, including race, to a unity in the Kingdom that nothing can disrupt.

What God is doing in the world today is beyond anything we are able to measure. Way beyond that! There is no measuring stick in the Scriptures that we can find, or even outside of it, to measure God's Kingdom power. We are simply called to have a God-faith, because He's going to do God things. Are you beginning to see it?

For Group Discussion:

For your opening session, spend some time introducing yourselves. Then discuss three or more of the questions below:

1. What point in this chapter stood out as most important to you? Why?

2. What kinds of authority are over you these days? What kinds of authority do you exercise over others?

3. According to the author, what is the nature of your authority in the Kingdom? How can you apply it in practical ways?

4. What is your approach to pastoral authority that goes wrong or seems immature? How can ordinary church members lovingly confront such a situation?

5. How does the idea of "being connected" in the Kingdom strike you? When have you been the most thankful for this connection?

6. What would it take for you to move one step ahead along the pathway of "turning your thinking around"?

7. What one area of repentance would you feel comfortable sharing with other group members? What prayer request do you have about this?

CHAPTER 2

Tempted, or Glowing?

(Based on Matthew 4:1-10)

Then was Jesus led up of the Spirit into the wilderness to be tempted of the devil.

—Matthew 4:1

The father of a small boy would sometimes sneak into a neighbor's orchard and pluck some of the choicest fruit. He always made sure, however, that "the coast was clear." One day, with his son tagging along, after carefully looking in every direction and seeing no one, he crept through the fence. He was just about ready to help himself when the youngster startled him by crying out, "Dad! Dad! You didn't look UP! You forgot to see if God is watching." [1]

It's true that God is always there. And though there are several good protections against temptation, the surest one is a cowardly response to the fact that you might get caught!

We can all relate to temptation. It hounds every one of us. In fact, it is only opportunity that knocks but once. Temptation pounds on the door constantly. And in the Gospel of Matthew we find that even Jesus is not immune to the Tempter's schemes. His response, however, is hardly cowardly.

You'll Be Tempted Like Him

If we want to face our temptations successfully, we do well to study the ways of Jesus when Satan approaches. In Matthew 4, when the Lord enters into ministry, He goes to the wilderness and immediately faces some subtle enticements. In similar fashion, when we are launching into ministry, we'll quickly face temptations. The following are three of the most powerful temptations we face.

1. Stones to Bread: Tempted to grab your power? In the first temptation of Jesus, Satan appears and says, "If you are the Son of God, turn these stones into bread." Now this is very subtle. And it's not just because Jesus was hungry. Nor is it simply a call to abuse His power. Rather, there's a subtlety to this temptation because Satan defeated the first Adam and has had four thousand years to plan his strategy to thwart the Last Adam (see 1 Corinthians 15:45). So when He recognizes that this is the moment, Satan uses the most intricate and refined methods.

You see, stones are a praise entity. Jesus once said, "If these people don't praise me, these stones will praise me." And we see stones in Ezekiel, where Satan walked between them. (I call this "God's Stock Exchange," because the stones would light up, and then Satan would trade what God wanted.) The words "these stones" can also carry us back to the story of the Jordan River crossing. There the people took twelve stones out of the river and they placed them on the bank, and the Lord said, "When your children ask, what do these stones mean? You will tell your children, '*These* stones represent Israel, who was taken out of Egypt.'" Of all the millions of stones in the River Jordan, only twelve were taken out. And *these* would symbolize that God chose His people particularly, before the foundation of the world, as a testimony that He is the One who blesses them.

So Satan was saying, change *these* stones into bread.

Of course, Jesus would not turn *these* stones, which are praise-entity stones, for a very good reason. It's because bread is a revelatory instrument. Bread always speaks of revelation. If Jesus turned stones into bread, then Satan could have gone to the court of justice in the Kingdom system and said, "God, I was once a praise agent, but I wanted to be promoted to a revelatory agent in the heavens. And because I tried that, I was banished. So, Christ now is disqualified and banished because He tried to turn a praise agent into a revelation agent." What a subtle approach in this temptation!

Then Jesus replies, "Man shall not live by bread alone." In other words, Satan, you missed the mark here. It's not by revelation; you have to live by the *proceeding*. It's a Word that is proceeding. It's continuation, it's contiguous, it's both line upon line, precept on precept. *Power in the spiritual life is an ongoing reliance upon the power of God.*

But today we are tempted to grab our own power. We experience a failure of faith and give in to doubt. What do we doubt? We question whether our God is a Father of good will toward us. We question whether He has our best at heart. We fear that, if there is any bread on the table, we may have to take it while the taking is good. Will God indeed supply? The answer is yes, according to Jesus. And the yes comes straight from the mouth of God. Will we let it proceed and take it into our being for daily nourishment?

2. Life to Death: Tempted to control your future?
The second temptation is similar to the first in its appeal
to our own sense of ability and control. Satan told Jesus
to throw Himself from the top of the Temple, because
they both knew that Jesus had the ability to keep
Himself from coming to any harm. He had the power to
control the situation, and the devil wanted to make him
use it.

For us, with no ability to control our life situations—
in the next day or even in the next moment—we are
tempted to act as if we should be able to save ourselves,
just in time. So it's important to ask: Am I the kind of person who needs to be sure of my next step before I take
it? Sure what the future will bring?

Let's think clearly about this. We can't even be sure of
our own internal motivations, can we? I like the way
writer Frederick Buechner put this in his book *The
Magnificent Defeat:* "The voice that we hear over our
shoulders never says, 'First be sure that your motives are
pure and selfless and then follow Me.' If it did, then we
could none of us follow. So when later the voice says,
'Take up your cross and follow me,' at least part of what
is meant by 'cross' is our realization that we are seldom
any less than nine parts fake. Yet our feet can insist on
answering Him anyway. And on we go, step after step."[2]

Faith faces the days ahead, one step at a time. Any
other approach to our future is an attempt, according to
the Scriptures, even to tempt God!

Think about the next tough decision you will face.
Will you attempt to "hedge your bets" with the Lord? Will
you try to control the unfolding of your future without
putting yourself before God in all your vulnerability to
say: "Here I am, Lord; use me as You will"?

Then we may be called to step forward, even while our motives are still forming themselves. Sometimes this means stepping into the dark, but not because we are tempted. Rather, we follow because we are aware of our sacred calling, our duty in the Kingdom. And this will not necessarily make the future smooth for us. As writer Madeleine L'Engle said: "We do not need the sheltering wings when things go smoothly. We are closest to God in the darkness, stumbling along blindly." To engage the riskiness of the future, then, is to trust God rather than tempt Him. It is to give Him the control of our lives.

3. Majesty to Machine: Tempted to settle for "life engineering"? This third temptation is so powerful because the Bible says Jesus was "taken *into* an exceeding high mountain," not *onto*. The reason He's taken into is that this word *mountain* is not just a peak. Here the word *mountain* comes from *basillia*, the Latin word meaning "a functional system." In other words, Jesus was taken into the *machine* of the enemy and tempted: "If You will worship me, I'll give You this machine."

Now watch Jesus' remarks here: "Get thee hence, Satan, for it is written thou shalt worship the Lord thy God and Him alone shalt thou serve." Notice Satan's terminology in the middle of a sentence: There's a capital A for all—*All* these things, because he was referring to something in particular that Jesus was shown. "All these things I will give to You if You will worship me." Jesus said, in effect, "Get out of here because I don't need to get all these things by worshiping you."

In Matthew 6:31, Jesus would say to us, "Seek ye first the Kingdom of Heaven and ALL these things shall be given to you as well." So Jesus was going to get all these things just by seeking the Kingdom. He was going to get it anyway. He didn't need some impy little devil to bow down and worship because Jesus was already designated to have it all. As are we.

But can we get it all by life engineering? Similar to attempting to control our future is the attempt to control our present. When each problem hits, we believe we can work a cure, find the fix, implement the plan. It is a subtle form of self-worship which, of course, is a bowing down to the Tempter himself.

Jesus didn't need to do it. He already had majesty, though He was "emptied" (see Philippians 2:6-8); with His power placed in the background, all His glory was there behind the scenes. The machine Satan offered was worthless in comparison to heavenly majesty, something already there.

The point for us is clear: *If you'll seek the Kingdom of God, whatever is a resource in your city has already been supplied to you.* That is, you must back Kingdom people and move forward with them. I don't care if it's a bank manager who's a God-hater, he can curse God in the morning, he can curse God for breakfast, lunch and supper. But when that bank manager comes face to face with you at the Kingdom, he must open his basilica to serve you!

So we will be tempted like Jesus. And, like Him, we can resist the powerful pull. An American named Rick Green wrote something that I'd like to share with you along these lines:

> A former policeman with whom I stayed on a choir tour told me about being on duty during an ice storm. The ice was a half-inch thick on every tree in the area. He was called to a site where the ice and

falling branches had caused a power line to come down; his duty was to keep people away from the area.

"There was a small tree near the fallen power line," he said, "the kind with a short trunk and lots of long thin branches. While that fallen power line was crackling and popping with electricity, it was throwing out sparks through the branches of that small tree. The sparks would reflect off the ice-covered branches sending out a rainbow of glimmering colors. I stood there and watched, and wondered how anything so beautiful could be so deadly."

I was reminded of the power of sin. We see something that seems beautiful, but when we reach out to touch, it becomes death to us.[3]

There are two ways to throw off sparks in the world, two ways to glow. Mr. Green saw how seemingly beautiful sin could be when it casts its multi-colored light upon the landscape. That is how temptation comes to us. Don't let it fool you. There is another way, a far-surpassing light that glows.

Will You Glow Like Him?
Come along as Jesus starts His ministry. The Scripture says that when He comes out of the wilderness (Matt. 4:12), Jesus leaves Nazareth and goes to Capernaum, which is by the seaside. He dwelt among the people of Zebulun and Naphtali, which are on the way to the sea, along the Jordan. "The people which sat in darkness saw great light; and to them which sat in the region and shadow of death light is sprung up" (4:16).

Now here is something important to see: that word "light" is a literal glowing. I've studied this extensively

to try to disprove what I thought the Scripture was saying, but I can't disprove it. So, Jesus was released in ministry, and He became a light. He literally began to glow.
Therefore, "the people that sat in darkness saw a great
light." It wasn't a symbolic illumination of wisdom or
knowledge. It wasn't just, "Oh, I see the light now; I
understand." No, when they looked at Him, they saw
Him glow.

And the folks came from everywhere to see this phenomenon. Even the disciples must have been amazed,
for when Jesus walked on the water, and they saw Him
in the middle of the night, we have to wonder: *how* did
they see Him? They said, "That's a spirit." How could
they see Him? Because He was *glowing*.

This is all very practical for you and me today. Yes,
we will be tempted with Jesus. *But will we glow with
Him, too?* A Kingdom church will glow with ministry,
with love, with giving, with preaching that strikes into
the heart, and with a movement in the Kingdom that
changes the world. We spend a lot of money on advertis-
ing, and there's probably nothing wrong with that. But if
you start glowing, you won't need to spend that money.
If you start glowing, the quality of your life will say it all.

For Group Discussion:

1. When do you seem most vulnerable to temptation these days? What is your typical "action plan" for resisting? What is most significant, for you, about the ways Jesus resisted?

2. What key idea in this chapter will help you most when temptation strikes next?

3. What is your personal experience with "grabbing power," "controlling the future," or "life engineering"? What advice would you give to a new believer experiencing any of these temptations?

4. Name some of the practical ways your church seems to "glow." In what areas could it shine even brighter in the future?

5. How would you characterize the "glow-level" of the Christians in your neighborhood or city? What things could be done to improve your Kingdom witness?

Notes:

1. Adapted from James S. Hewett, ed., Illustrations Unlimited (Wheaton, IL: Tyndale House Publishers, 1988), p. 477.

2. Frederick Buechner, The Magnificent Defeat (San Francisco: Harper Books, 1985), np.

3. Adapted from Craig Brian Larson, ed., Illustrations for Preaching and Teaching (Grand Rapids, MI: Baker Books, 1993), p. 241.

CHAPTER 3

Salt and Light–Take Over!

(Based on Matthew 5—6)

Ye are the light of the world.
A city that is set on an hill cannot be hid.
—Matthew 5:14

The Bible says that Jesus, seeing the multitudes, began preaching. And the people came from everywhere to hear Him. They came from Galilee, from out of the ten cities of Decapolis, from Jerusalem, from Judea, and from beyond the Jordan River to the east. They seemed to know, even without telephones, without e-mail, without CNN, that this was a man to be heard. "You gotta come see what's happening in this place! Some man is glowing here!"

And just by the light of His being shining amidst the darkness—the physical sickness and spiritual hunger—people were dramatically transformed. And why not? They saw a light that hadn't been manifest in all the years down through four millenniums. The same light that walked in the Garden of Eden with Adam suddenly came amongst human beings and brought order and power. So, when He saw the multitudes, "He went up into a mountain: and when He was set . . . He opened His mouth" (5:1-2).

From His mouth flowed the culture-countering beatitudes found in Matthew 5:3-10. And from His mouth came the encouraging words to the persecuted in verses 11 and 12. Then, in verses 13-16, He spoke directly to these people (and us) about their identity in the Kingdom and what it ought to mean to them. As you'll see, in the Kingdom, you and I have two kinds of *influence* (salt and light) and two kinds of *power* (prayer and protocol). How will we use them in a Kingdom that is moving, expanding, and spreading God's new ways across the earth?

Be Aware: You Are Salt and Light

Someone asks: "Who are you?"

How do you respond? Do you simply give your name? Do you begin speaking about your job? Do you tell about your grandchildren? Or would you let Jesus define you and say: "Basically, I'm salt and light in God's Kingdom"? If that is your primary identity, it's time to learn about what it means—and what it calls you to do.

Salt: By your all-pervading influence, "flavor" your city. You can have a pot full of meat, add a small amount of salt, and that entire pot will fall under a flavorful influence. Naturally, you don't add salt in an amount equal to the weight of the meat. You sprinkle in a proportionate amount of salt according to your taste. So if you have meat that weighs four pounds, you don't add four pounds of salt. It has much more influence than just one-to-one.

"You are salt," Jesus says. Therefore, the potency of the Kingdom of God is such that if you, as a lesser influence, go into a building of ungodly people where there might be a hundred people who don't serve the Lord, you will eventually bring the entire building of people under your influence.

You can be in a school, in a classroom, serving God on your own. And you might think, "Oh, there are so many people here who don't love God." But remember the potency of your strength in the Kingdom. If you're placed into a pot with a bunch of devils, sooner or later you will bring the entire place under your own influence for God's glory. Daniel did it. Elisha did it. Elijah did it. Joseph did it. David did it. And you can do it if you understand the potency of the Kingdom of God. Just be a little bit of salt, and you can change a nation.

What does this mean to you? First, *it's why a church like yours has to be salt.* If we are going to be an influence in the nation of Zimbabwe or in the nation of the United States or the nation of the United Kingdom, all God is looking for is a church, a ministry that has a Kingdom mentality. If that Kingdom mentality can start in the house, it will affect the city, and eventually it will affect the nation. You cannot add a grain of salt to a piece of meat without that meat being affected.

And Jesus' words about salt have a very personal application, too. *It's why some of you have been called, as individuals, to difficult places.* You see, we could picture God as perfection itself; with salt, that means a perfect cube. If you break that cube into various pieces—the children of God in the Kingdom— it always breaks into more complete cubes. Therefore, God's person, wherever he or she is, manifests the length, breadth, and height of the Kingdom. This person is, in a sense, the holiest of holies in the darkest places on earth! For in this person, God's government resides in that place. It's where the totality of God's experience is. Do you see your importance as a church, or even as a single, lonely witness in the "outback" of God's creation?

So if God takes you as Kingdom salt, and places you in a city, it's just a matter of time before the whole area will come under your influence. You are the salt of the earth! You can be placed in the middle of a crackhouse, in the middle of a drug-infested community. You can enter into the heart of Sodom, amidst homosexuality, day in and day out. It's just a matter of time before the influence starts.

In other words, as salt, *we're taking over!* Everything the devil sows, we're taking over. We're just going to put some Kingdom salt into it. We're bringing it all under the King's influence.

Light: By combining your candles, light up the entire hill! Jesus says, "You are the light of the world." But then He goes to the next level, which is "a city that sits on a hill." So first is the Kingdom, the light of the world, then comes the city on a hill. Then comes the house. "Neither do men light a candle." Well, that's ridiculous. How many men do you need to light a candle? It only takes one individual to light a candle. But it says, "neither do men light a candle, and put it under a bushel, but on a candlestick."

So let's think clearly about all of these messages coming to us in Matthew 5:14-16. There's the house. That's why your "house"—your local church—and all the other houses in your area have to be together. Because *it takes a group of men to start a light of vision.* Do you see what I mean? Men and women have to light their candles and say, "We are a light in the city. Our house is going to be a light in the city." When you have *this* house alight

with people of vision who light that candle over there
. . . and in your house, *these* people of vision light *this*
candle . . . eventually a city—suddenly, with all these
houses with Kingdom lights—will shine out from the
hill with Kingdom glory.

We have so many churches in various cities, but
they never get to the next level, which is to be a light on
a hill, a city on a hill. We have a lot of people trying to
light up the whole world. Yet they're struggling with trying to get the candle lit in the house.

Notice that there are three levels in this passage: the
house, the city, the Kingdom. We'll talk much more
about this in Chapter 5. But here, I just want to make
this point: If you have a house setting, like a church, *it
takes corporate vision in that house to move with the
Kingdom.* It calls for men and women who are willing
to put aside their personal agendas, who can come
together to light the corporate house vision. When
these men and women in a church, in a ministry, light
this candle, then this candle becomes an influence in
the house. So in a church, depending on the size, as the
candle is lit, that candle cannot try to light a city on its
own.

So our vision, our candle, our ministry, must join
then with another ministry that is a candle. And that
ministry must work with other ministries within the
city until we have ten or twenty strong churches in a
city that are willing to come together. That's the only
time you have a city set on a hill.

Simply put, one church is not enough to take a city.
It has to be a unity of churches, especially in the twenty-first century. There have to be several candles lighting the rooms.

This is so very real to me. A number of years ago I was in Newark, New Jersey, preaching a conference at Symphony Hall. It was a wonderful place, but the whole approach of the group was less than wonderful. It could be summarized like this: "We start church at 7:30, sing until about half past 10:00, get the preacher up at 11:00, preach the fool out of himself and everybody else, and then go out at 1:00 in the morning to eat and then, eventually, go back to the hotel. Sleep all day, get up at about 2:00 in the afternoon, have a bite to eat, and get ready for church that night."

That was how the entire seven-day conference was supposed to work.

I remember coming back to the hotel one night at 2:30 A.M. I came out of the shower, getting ready for bed, and the Lord spoke: "Build a strong base."

I had no idea what He meant. But the Lord spoke again and said, "I'm going to teach you." And that night I received the first step of strategy towards building what our ministry is becoming. Because God wants first *houses that are candles*. "Thy word is a lamp unto my feet." That must manifest.

Also, "The steps of a good man are ordered." How are they ordered? When the light goes before them. You see, there are a lot of people in the dark because they haven't lit the Kingdom candle to order their steps. After all, we don't have the sense even to find our hotel room, if it weren't for God.

Beware: You Need Prayer and Protocol

To fulfill the calling of our identity in the Kingdom, we need to ask things of God (in prayer), and we need to ask *properly* (by protocol). In Matthew 6, in the middle of this discourse, Jesus gives us what we call the Lord's

Prayer. He says something crucial here: When we pray, we are to say: "Thy Kingdom come. Thy will be done on earth, as it is in heaven." He's now beginning to release, in essence, the Kingdom in the not-too-distant future. When you pray (that's future), say "the establishment of the Kingdom" because there's going to be tremendous resistance to the establishing of this Kingdom.

Then Jesus deals with something in 6:19 which I call headship release: He says here that we ought not to label ourselves as "treasures on earth." I've heard this preached so many times to prove that we're supposed to be poor—but this has nothing to do with that theme. Jesus is dealing with the dynamics of protocol.

He's addressing people here, releasing the level of the Kingdom. He's saying that you've got to aim high and begin to lay up treasures in the Kingdom of God, because here on earth our treasures are corrupted. He was no doubt referring to the many marauding forces that had come through Israel, from the time of their establishment in the Promised Land. There had been so many conquering forces, like Nebuchadnezzar, coming in and raiding and taking the treasures of that earthly kingdom.

So Jesus says, in effect, "Don't lay up treasures in the old way you used to do it. No, begin to aim higher, because there's a higher level of storing treasures." Israel's people, when they lost their treasures on the earth, were totally bankrupt. But if we lay up treasures on a higher level, then never mind the theft of our stuff here on earth. There's something up there that the devil cannot touch!

"For where your treasure is, there will your heart

be also." It's true! There's an old story illustrating it well. It's said that a rich woman dreamed she went to heaven and saw there a mansion being built. "Who is that for?" she asked of the guide.

"For your gardener."

"But on earth he lives in the tiniest cottage, with barely room enough for his family. He might live better if he didn't give so much to the miserable, poor folk."

Farther on she saw a tiny cottage being built. "And who is that for?" she asked.

"That is for you."

"But I've lived in a mansion on earth. I wouldn't know how to live in a cottage."

The words she heard in reply were full of meaning: "The Master Builder is doing His best with the material that is being sent up."

Enough said?

Now Jesus reveals headship gifts. He says, "The light of the body is the eye"—in other words, levels of headship are coming. And the most important of the headship gifts is the eye. If you don't have headship gifts that can see, the whole body is going to be dark. That's why, in a city like yours and mine, where God is bringing us together, somebody in that place is the eye. To see, to give light to Omaha, or Newark, or Tampa. Somebody else is the ear, somebody else is the taste, and the whole body has to work together to bring a completeness to the body in a particular region—even in a house, even in the city, even in the Kingdom.

Finally, Jesus says: "If you seek the Kingdom first, then all these things will be added unto you." The Kingdom is so powerful you won't have to worry about being furnished with physical things. You won't have to worry about clothes, or food, or money. God knows you need these things, and they will be provided for you. For when you step into the Kingdom, those things are already there. Just keep praying and submitting to the protocol of the Kingdom. Just keep being salt to flavor your house, your city, your whole world. Just keep glowing by reflecting the only true source of radiance that ever came into the world: ALL GLORY TO YOU, LORD CHRIST!

For Group Discussion:

1. In your opinion, what is the author's main reason for emphasizing our identity in the Kingdom?

2. What does it mean to you, in practical terms, to be salt and light in your world? When do you feel you are doing a good job of this? How would you like to improve?

3. Why is it so crucial for Christians and churches to come together? When have you seen this happening with good results? What are some of the most difficult obstacles to "lighting the candles" together in your city?

4. How would you describe the state of your prayer life these days? What main teaching here about prayer is most relevant to your life right now?

5. What does the author mean by "protocol" and "headship gifts"? When have you seen these in action?

6. What key personal application is here for you in this chapter?

7. How would you like others to pray for you this week?

CHAPTER 4

Build the Kingdom with Holy Work

(Based on Matthew 8—10)

Then saith he unto his disciples, The harvest truly is plenteous, but the labourers are few; Pray ye therefore the Lord of the harvest, that He will send forth labourers.

—Matthew 9:37-38

Long ago, before Western colonialists imposed national boundaries, the kings of Laos and Vietnam reached an agreement about how to tax the border areas. Those families who ate short-grain rice, built their houses on stilts, and decorated them with Indian-style serpents were considered Laotians. On the other hand, those who ate long-grain rice, built their houses on the ground, and decorated them with Chinese-style dragons were considered Vietnamese.[1]

The exact *location* of a person's home wouldn't determine national identity. No, *culture* would determine it. Each person belonged to the kingdom whose cultural values he or she exhibited.

Keep this in mind as you consider the idea that it takes work to build a kingdom, even to build the Kingdom of Heaven. In Matthew 9 and 10, Jesus shows us how He'll build His Kingdom—which is less a matter of geographical expansion than a matter of *spreading certain values that transform the values of society's status quo*. Jesus uses at least three means to do this holy work: by doing it Himself, by doing it through His disciples, and even by doing it through the angels.

Doing Holy Work Himself

In Matthew 8, Jesus is going to preach the Kingdom and demonstrate how He's going to build it. Naturally, He leads in doing the work. The first thing He does is to heal a leper, then a centurion's servant, then Peter's mother-in-law. His work continues until we come to the middle of chapter 9, where three miracles of extreme significance stand out to us:

A Girl: Awakening what was dying (18-26). Jesus healed a ruler's daughter, a girl who had been sick for twelve years. The father had said, "She died." Jesus said she was only sleeping. This was a sign given to Israel, that Israel was a dying entity and that the foundational structure, which is twelve in the Kingdom of God, was dying. Now God had come to resuscitate it by raising it up. It wasn't dead; it was just sleeping. He had come to awaken what was dying.

A Woman: Making productive what was unproductive (20-22). As Jesus went to heal the young girl, a woman who had suffered with bleeding for twelve years clutched the hem of His garments. When she touched him, her reproductive system, which had been dead or unproductive, received life in it. Now the womb that could not produce life, which was Israel, was going to be opened to be the first release of the Kingdom that was coming. So Jesus heals the reproductive system in the Kingdom.

Some Men: Opening what was closed (27-34). Then comes the third miracle, in which Jesus heals the blind and casts out devils from a man who was mute. He opens the closed eyes and the closed mouth. In Israel, through His words and deeds, through bringing the Kingdom, Jesus will open minds and hearts as well.

Then the Scripture says: "When He saw the multitude, He was so moved with compassion" because there were people who had no shepherds, people who were just scattered. Jesus said to His disciples, "The harvest is plenteous, the labors are few, pray you, therefore, for the Lord of the harvest, that He might send laborers into the harvest."

We need to pray that prayer today. Work is waiting to be done.

Doing Holy Work—Through Others

Yes, the fields beckon us, because Jesus enlists laborers that He might work through them. He doesn't do all the work directly; He does some of it indirectly through others. His power alone is the effective agent. Yet human beings—the disciples of the past and the followers of today—are blessed with the privilege of being holy conduits.

Jesus does His work through the original followers. In Matthew 10, Jesus commissions the first disciples and sends them. Chapter 10 is what I call "The Apostles' Manual." We see, for example, that Jesus gives these followers power against unclean spirits and power over disease. And then the Scripture says, "He named His twelve disciples"—so He names them in the order of their rank—and then He says to them, "Don't go to the Gentiles"—because that's the next level. He says, "First, go to the house of Israel." We're going to start by building *this* house. That's where I'm sending you.

He says, "When you go, preach the Kingdom of God," because the Kingdom of God is built in such a way that it's going to manifest what we find in verse 8: Heal the sick, cleanse the lepers, raise the dead, cast out devils. Freely receive, freely give. Don't take gold or silver, because that's already provided for you.

So Jesus is saying that when you begin to preach the Kingdom and you start building the house of Israel, the sick are going to be healed, lepers cleansed, dead raised, all these kinds of things will start happening to herald a brand new reign upon the earth, God's reign.

Jesus wants to do His work through YOU today. There is so much in Matthew 10 but let's pick up in verse 24: Jesus says, "The disciple is not above his master, nor the servant above his lord." He was saying that "I am your master and you are a servant serving Me. You can never be above Me, but you can be equal to Me."

You are a servant of the Lord if you know Him as Savior. He wants to work through you just as He worked through those original followers so many centuries ago. So I'd like to ask you to consider certain "servant principles" that can help you be the best servant possible. I'm going to list six of them that flow from the rest of the verses in Matthew 10. Are you ready?

• Servant Principle #1: Know your gift and look above it (verse 24). It's important that you know your gift and know you're anointed when God sends you into a place. Because the people in that place will only rise to the level of the leader's anointing. That's why we need levels of leadership above us, because if we are serving a house, like I am serving a church in Zimbabwe, those people I serve can only be as strong as the anointing that God has entrusted to me. If I don't have anybody above me, that's the only level we'll ever experience. But if I have somebody above me that I serve, then we go to the next level, and they come to that level with me. So Jesus says, "You are not going to be above your master."

• Servant Principle #2: Get used to being called names (verse 25). Jesus tells you that whatever they call your master, they will call you. "They call Me a devil, so don't be surprised if they call you a devil."

But there's a positive aspect to this. If they call Jesus "Son of David, with tender mercies," then that's the same thing that they'll call you. If they call Him "prosperous," then you're going to be called prosperous. If they call Him "blessed," then you're going to be called "blessed." So whatever the Lord is called in a city, the devil may use people to call you those things.

But then you have to ask yourself: "What does God say about me?" Because what God says about you affects the entire city.

That's why you have to know what God calls you, you have to know what title God has put on your life. If God has called you a "devil disturber," everybody in your church will have the same kind of mandate you have.

• Servant Principle #3: Never let fear stop you; God will supply (verse 26). When you come to the next level of growth, you're in the dark. That's when yesterday's level is your greatest strength. But you are now very weak on this higher level. That's why you are weak, but yet you're strong.

Jesus says when you come to the next level, anything covered will be revealed. In other words, when God promotes you to the next level, and you confront everything that seems hidden to you, then God will lift the covers up and say you will have now what you need to function here. God is not going to hide anything from you. He's going to show you everything you need to know in order to carry out your Kingdom mandate.

• Servant Principle #4: Draw upon divine power, even amidst shadows (verse 27). "What I tell you in darkness, speak in the light. What you hear in the ear, preach from the housetops." In other words, this is a headship anointing. If you infect the leadership, it will go all the way down to the basement. The weakest one in the Kingdom is greater. "I'm going to empower you; what you hear in darkness, what I speak to you in the secret place—shall abide in the shadow of the Almighty."

In other words, there are times when God has to keep you in the shadow, which is called darkness. And the shadow is great. Look what happens in the shadow:

> He that dwelleth in the secret place of the most High shall abide under the SHADOW of the Almighty. I will say of the LORD, He is my refuge and my fortress: my God; in him will I trust. Surely he shall deliver thee from the snare of the fowler, and from the noisome pestilence.
>
> He shall cover thee with his feathers, and under his wings shalt thou trust: his truth shall be thy shield and buckler. Thou shalt not be afraid for the terror by night; nor for the arrow that flieth by day; Nor for the pestilence that walketh in dark-

ness; nor for the destruction that wasteth at noonday.

A thousand shall fall at thy side, and ten thousand at thy right hand; but it shall not come nigh thee. Only with thine eyes shalt thou behold and see the reward of the wicked. Because thou hast made the LORD, which is my refuge, even the most High, thy habitation; There shall no evil befall thee, neither shall any plague come nigh thy dwelling.

For he shall give his angels charge over thee, to keep thee in all thy ways. They shall bear thee up in their hands, lest thou dash thy foot against a stone. Thou shalt tread upon the lion and adder: the young lion and the dragon shalt thou trample under feet.

Because he hath set his love upon me, therefore will I deliver him: I will set him on high, because he hath known my name.

—Psalm 91:1-14

My brother and sister, if the shadow is so glorious, think of what's going to happen when God brings you into the light!

• Servant Principle #5: Always trust God's season (verse 30). In speaking of hairs, Jesus is talking about seed—every seed in the Kingdom of God. Every seed, every cell, has a biological DNA number that's recorded in the heavenly computer. The Lord knows when a sparrow dies and He's there to harvest it. Every living organism, every cell, is numbered. So when the devil steals a seed, he hasn't really stolen that seed because he doesn't have the patience for that. He is possessing it illegally, and the angels will say, "One seed that

Johnson sowed has gone astray."

God keeps a record of that, because when God puts His fear on the enemy, that seed that was stolen is numbered. It hasn't shown up as fruitful. And He commanded every seed, in Genesis 1:11, to "be fruitful, and bring forth after its kind." So it's not fruitful, and therefore hasn't shown up in the heavenly computer. In effect, God says "If you will not faint, in due season, you shall reap." Whatever you sow, you shall reap. Don't faint, because you're going to reap if you sow the seed that's coming.

• <u>Servant Principle #6: Recognize the other's gifts— and receive (verse 40).</u> "He that receiveth you receiveth Me, and he that receiveth Me receiveth Him that sent Me." In other words, we have to recognize each other's gifts. "If you receive the gift I send"—if that city will receive you—"then you'll receive everything that I come with." If you receive a gift from the city, God will make sure that the nation of Christ will be formed in you. He that starts the good work in you will be faithful to complete it.

Doing Holy Work —Even through Angels

My friend, there's an angel who has been given a mandate in the city where you live. That mandate is the Kingdom mandate. This Kingdom mandate is so important that he's been given instructions as to what the will of God is for your region. Every house has an angelic prince over that house that reports to the angel over the city. If you speak bad about him, the angels in your house will stand and not fight for you. You're working in the realm of man, and the angels will not fight for you. They will not bring provisions for you, they will not bring money for you. Your angels and my angels work together, fighting on the same front so that your city can accept more!

In one place in Scripture, Jesus says, "Rejoice, because you have been recorded as a Kingdom bearer." Do you like the sound of that? Do you see yourself as a Kingdom bearer in your home, in your neighborhood, in your city?

As for me, I'd rather have my name recorded as a Kingdom bearer than anything else. As Kingdom bearers we remove the devil. As Kingdom bearers, there's nothing stopping us, nothing impossible for us to accomplish through the mighty arm of the King himself. With human power alone, nothing comes to pass. But with God all things are possible, every day.

For Group Discussion:

1. Why does building the Kingdom take work? What kind of work?

2. How has Jesus worked through you in the past? How would you like him to work in and through you in the future?

3. Of the six "servant principles," which speaks to you most powerfully? Why?

4. Have you ever considered the role of angels in advancing the Kingdom? What are some practical implications of this teaching?

5. What does it mean to you to be a "Kingdom bearer"?

Chapter 4 Notes

1. Story told by John Hess-Yoder, in Craig Brian Larson, ed., Illustrations for Preaching and Teaching (Grand Rapids, MI: Baker Books, 1993), p. 125

CHAPTER 5

The House, the City, the Kingdom

(Based on Matthew 12:22-30)

He that is not with me is against me;
and he that gathereth not with me scattereth
abroad.

—Matthew 12:30

Strong individuals form strong families, which make strong churches. Strong churches influence cities, which influence nations, bringing God's Life into the world for His glory. Do you see this progression and how important it is?

Let's be very practical about it: The reason there's unemployment in a nation, the reason there's sickness and conflict in a nation, is not just because of bad government. Part of the reason is that the church isn't doing its job. If the church was doing everything it's supposed to do—if it was the salt of the earth, the light of the world—imagine the difference in society! If we have strong churches that have lit candles and are joined together, then we can claim the Bible's promise: "Yet have I not seen the righteous forsaken, nor his seed begging bread" (Psalm 37:25).

If the churches would be the Church, we would create jobs because God would make sure that people were employed. God would make sure that people were fed and clothed. But it starts with being a strong person, individually. Then being a strong family. Then gathering families to produce strong churches.

Jesus Demonstrates This Process

All of this is in the Gospel of Matthew. And what I touched on in Matthew 12 (in the first chapter of this book), I now want to expand upon here. Recall that Jesus is going to demonstrate the Kingdom of God to His apostles. He begins by giving them power and authority against unclean spirits in Matthew 10. Then, in chapters 11 and 12, He begins to demonstrate what He's just given them. So in Matthew 12 we find what I call the "Miracles of the Seventh Day." These miracles will show to them that they are going to have power against all odds.

One of the miracles of the seventh day is that Jesus delivers a young boy possessed with a devil, a blind and dumb spirit. This boy couldn't see and he couldn't speak. So the people were amazed when they saw the boy made whole, yet the Pharisees said, "This Jesus is casting out devils by the prince of devils."

But Jesus "knew their thoughts." And by knowing their thoughts He makes this incredible statement: "Every Kingdom divided against itself is brought to desolation." That's the ultimate level, the Kingdom. Then He says, "Every city or house." So here you have the other levels, the city and the house. So very plainly, you have the house, the city, and the Kingdom.

In light of this crucial pronouncement by Jesus, here is what I want to say to you in this chapter: If you're going to see the Kingdom come—God glorified across the earth—you'll travel through three *dimensions of function* and six *stages of operation*.

The dimensions are: house, city, and Kingdom. Please realize that I will use the terms "house," "city," and "kingdom" to refer to various different entities in this chapter. They are expressions, or dimensions of function that can characterize forms of relationship. Hopefully, this will become clear as you continue reading.

The six stages are described below. Analyze them carefully to see where you and your church fit in (and what your next step can be).

Stage #1. Being an individual of committed passion for Christ. Recall that in Matthew 5 Jesus said, "You are the light of the world. A city set on a hill cannot be hid. Neither do men light a candle in a house." The first "house" that we have—and remember that I speak of several levels of houses—is simply the individual believer. The Bible says that your body is the temple of the Holy Spirit. So you, as a person, are a house. The Holy Spirit dwells in you. The Bible says that the candle, or spirit of a man, is the candle of the Lord.

So you are a house. And if you're going to move from a house-level of witness to a city-level, how do you do it? I'll use my wife, ChiChi, and I as an example. Individually, we are each a house. She lights a candle in her house, and I light a candle in my house. How do we light that candle? Well, the Word of God is a light and a lamp, so we've got to get the Word into us deeply, in all wisdom. We let the Word of God dwell in us. As Jesus said, it's not what goes into a person that defiles him, but what comes out.

Now this is a very down-to-earth thing for each Christian believer—to become Word-oriented, day-by-day and moment-by-moment. It simply requires a constant re-focusing of the mind on the spiritual realities as we go about our routines. Here is how the great British writer and teacher C.S. Lewis once put it:

> The real problem of the Christian life comes where people do not usually look for it. It comes the very moment you wake up each morning. All your wishes and hopes for the day rush at you like wild animals. And the first job each morning consists simply in shoving them all back; in listening to that other voice, taking that other point of view, letting that other larger, stronger, quieter life come flowing in, and so on, all day. Standing back from all your natural fussings and frettings; coming in out of the wind.
>
> We can only do it for moments at first. But from those moments the new sort of life will be spreading through our system: because now we are letting Him work at the right part of us. It is the difference between paint, which is merely laid on the surface, and a dye or stain that soaks right through.[1]

Can you come in out of the wind during your days? If so, you are learning to "build your house" on the foundation of God's Word. That is what ChiChi and I want to do. The Word lights the candle of our spirit in our house.

Stage #2. Growing a family of neighborly influence. When ChiChi and I got married, we then left the house setting and came into the city setting, because now we had two candles set on a hill that could not be hid. So when you look at ChiChi and me, you're looking at a city and not necessarily a house. And when we had children, then we moved from two candles to many candles, in our case, four boys. So we moved from an individual house to a city (marriage), and then from a city to a Kingdom (children). By the way our family lives, we can influence an entire neighborhood just by being a Kingdom family. Is that the way it is with your family?

The Bible says a man cannot be a bishop if he doesn't rule his family-house well. Author James Dobson puts it like this for the people of the USA:

> If America is going to survive the incredible stresses and dangers it now faces, it will be because husbands and fathers again place their families at the highest level on their system of priorities, reserving a portion of their time and energy for leadership within their homes.[2]

It seems that men, especially, are called to light a candle in their homes. We men are an example in our own home as a "house."

Stage #3. Combining families for a strong church.

If we go to the third level, a local church then becomes the "house." The Bible uses expressions like this: "It was the house of David, or Abraham's household, or the house of Jacob." It means that the particular corporate family or church family was the house.

When our family comes to church now, we then enter into the next level, which is the city. You have the Bismark house, the Bernard house, etc., that come in with their own candles, and all the candles in that first dimension of the house light up the whole place into a city level. The church now, corporately with all these individual houses, becomes the city. Now when you take a good church with strong families shining candles, and you bring it into a city like Chicago or Houston, we then now qualify to enter into the

Kingdom. I am simply speaking here of a progression of excellence, of going to the next level, of improving. This is the Kingdom in motion.

And how does a strong church look? At the least, it has diverse ministries that are meeting peoples' needs in many ways. I say diverse because the needs in Zimbabwe, for instance, may not be the same needs that are in Cameroon, or Argentina, or the USA. The needs that are in Japan may not be the same needs that arise in Germany. The needs in Sweden are not the needs you find in Canada. Each city, each nation, has different needs, so God has to tailor-make those ministries to meet them. That's why Zechariah said: "Craftsmen are set to build the house."

We cannot try to duplicate what some church is doing in Zambia. We can go to that church and get some ideas, but we'd be foolish to try to duplicate that exact ministry to meet our own particular needs. We have different cultures, a different ethnos, therefore we have to trust the Holy Spirit to tailor-make this house with rooms to meet the needs in this nation.

My heart, of course, beats with a passion for Africa, and Africa is facing an AIDS epidemic. So we cannot try to import what Dr. Cho is doing in Korea, and he shouldn't try to import what we are trying to do here to meet human needs. God builds the house as we follow him to become strong.

Stage #4. Gathering churches for a witnessing city.

Now we take this church-house, with its strong message and ministry—where people must pay their bills, live with integrity, walk away from corruption, keep themselves sexually pure—and we combine it with other churches. Once we come together on that level, now it's city-level.

So when churches pray together, individual candles come together in the city. Remember—the Bible says that a city that's set on a hill cannot be hid. The demonstration on that level goes throughout a nation. In fact, people all over the region hear about it.

And when pastors come together and they say they are going to make time to be together, they are coming together as men to light a candle in their city. There is power in this kind of witness that works in superhuman ways. One person said it like this· "To be a witness does not consist in engaging in propaganda, nor even in stirring people up; but in being a living mystery. It means to live in such a way that one's life would not make sense if God did not exist."

How does all of this happen? We put aside our individual agendas for the corporate good. We willingly bring our local church program into the "program"— the will of God—for our city.

Such churches, the ones who work together, are on a mission. They're not just a bunch of people who get together on Sunday to sing and preach—that's not good enough. We can't just be a strong church on one side of town. Instead, make sure that if you're on the south side, you hook up with a church on the north side, which joins up with a church on the east side, which embraces a congregation on the west side. When you have this compass of joining together, you can then influence an entire city.

Stage #5. Bringing cities together for a God-honoring nation.

So we light a candle that is called the "House of Harare," the "House of Dallas," the "House of

Jerusalem." When the leaders come together and light that candle, they build a strong house in the city. If Houston then lights its house, Dallas lights its house, New York, Los Angeles, Detroit—all of these cities light their house—you can move the nation in a Kingdom level.

Human governments don't have the power to bring the kind of change God's Kingdom can bring. One man—Daniel—brought an entire nation to its knees through his testimony. If one man can do it without the Bible, without the Holy Ghost, without the kind of gifts we have today, then think of what individuals, families, churches, cities, and nations can do in the unity of the Spirit.

Stage #6. Bringing nations together for a world that glorifies its Creator.

Then let's take it a step further. Consider a nation like Zimbabwe or a nation like Zambia, where you have all these cities forming one nation. Now the nation can come unto God and say, "We are now going to join the level where a whole nation is actually a 'house.' We all agree in the cities, our churches, all the way down to our families, all the way down to individuals, and we bring all these levels together as a Zimbabwean nation, and we light a candle. It's then that the Zimbabwean House can join with the Zambian House, or join with the Nigerian House, or the Ugandan House. All of these houses coming together will now begin to enter into the city level and then we can begin to influence Africa. This country now is doing well as a church, or a "house."

Now we come to a city level at this stage. The Bible says when you come to a city level, you cannot be hid, right? Once we are together, as a continent, on a city level, we can then come together on a Kingdom level.

That is, all the African people agree and are now joined together. Once we, as African people agree, then we can join with the South American House, the North American House, the European House, the Asian House, the Australian house. When you have all of these "houses"—which are now entire continents on this level coming together—now the whole world is going to be filled with the glory of the Lord as the waters cover the sea!

The Challenge Is Great

Are we ever going to conquer the power of the Islamic movement in the world? (There are over a billion Muslims in the world, and the religion is spreading daily.) And how in the world are we going to spread the Gospel of Jesus Christ when we're dealing with a Hindu nation that is so vast, almost 800,000,000 strong? What about the vast numbers of adherents to Shintoism and Buddhism, and all the other world religions? How is the Gospel of Jesus Christ going to have impact?

The way it's going to happen, Jesus said, is by a progression: It starts with you and me. Individuals. Seeking to be a strong Christian as a man, as a woman. Let the light of God shine in your spirit. Do everything in your power to reach out in love. And overcome your fear of speaking for the Lord. William A. Ward[3] said:

"Fight the temptation to be bashful about the Christian faith. Avoid a bashful brand of Christianity that tiptoes up to people and hesitatingly suggests: "I may be wrong, but I'm afraid that if you do not repent after a fashion and receive Christ, so to speak, you might be damned, as it were."

No, we must be bold, plain, and direct in our witness. That's why Paul said, "Be strong in the Lord and in the power of His might." Because a strong man produces a strong Christian testimony as an individual. God will hook that man up with a strong woman. Together they will build a strong family. Strong families make strong churches. Strong churches in cities influence the social dynamics of those cities. Strong cities transform an entire nation. Strong nations can bring Light and Life into the world. And, ultimately, all glory will go to God, which is the supreme goal of the Kingdom in motion.

For Group Discussion:

1. Together review the six stages of Kingdom operation. Where do you fit in—as an individual, a church member, a citizen?

2. How would you describe the quality of your family witness these days?

3. What is your church doing to reach out to other congregations in your area? What ideas do you have to help encourage this?

4. When have you seen a person, family, or church "that could not be hid"? How did this affect you?

5. To what extent are you inspired by the vision of an entire world that brings glory to God? Talk about it!

6. What prayer requests would you like to share with the other group members?

Notes: Chapter 5

1. C.S. Lewis, Mere Christianity (New York: Macmillan Publishing, 1962).

2. James Dobson, Straight Talk to Men and Their Wives (Grand Rapids: Word Publishing, 1987).

3. William A. Ward, quoted in Lloyd Cory, ed., Quote, Unquote (Wheaton, IL: Scripture Press, 1977)

CHAPTER 6:

Wake Up and Boldly Move with God

(Based on Matthew 13:1-30; 36-43)

While men slept, his enemy came and sowed tares among the wheat, and went his way.
—Matthew 13:25

"What is faith?" asked the Sunday School teacher.

A young boy answered in a flash, "Believing something you know isn't true."

Do we sometimes think that way, even as adults? If you've found yourself questioning the goodness of God toward you, I want to encourage you in the faith. As you awaken your heart, as you open it up to the deep relationship Jesus wants, your faith will grow—in spite of hard times, in the midst of sleepless nights, and through the dark valleys. He is there with you in all those places. He grows your faith as you give Him control.

My own faith has been wonderfully fortified in recent days by a young man who came to our church from Nigeria. He was traveling to Europe, and to the struggling parts of Asia and South America, to preach the Kingdom of God. In his crusade in Mexico City last year, amidst all of the healings that took place, it was even reported that five bodies were raised from the dead when the Lord came in. It was a powerful demonstration of the power of God, because the Kingdom of God was there.

This young man said to me, "I am so ruthless with my faith now. If people come with blind eyes to the crusade, that's just child's play. If you can believe God for the dead being raised, then blind eyes are nothing." Then he made this statement that I hope will pervade this entire chapter: "It's the Word that produces faith, Bishop. And faith produces confidence. And confidence produces boldness."

I add this: *Boldness manifests the Kingdom.*

Can you believe God for incredible things? I'm at the point of ruthless faith, too. I'm getting to the stage now where it's almost impossible to have unbelief.

And yet it is a dangerous thing to try to generate faith on our own, as the young man reminds us. We may end up being religious but in rebellion toward heaven. We may be wide awake to tradition but asleep to God. That's why Jesus, with his parables in Matthew 13, sought to awaken his hearers' faith by teaching them how to think clearly about the things of God.

And this much ought to be clear to everyone who hears: As God's favor and preference continue to unfold, then change and progress will characterize the Kingdom. We must move with it; however, we must also guard against our enemy and every faith-quenching influence. A humanly pious mindset and the Kingdom of God are two different things. You can be in the Kingdom of God today; tomorrow you may be merely religious.

In Matthew 13 Jesus tells seven parables. But I want to focus on two that have critical importance for us in the church today, we who so desperately need to move forward with bold faith: the Parable of the Sower—regarding how faith takes root; and the Parable of the Wheat and Tares—regarding how faith can be subtly, but fatally, diluted.

The Sown Seed: God's Preference Will Progress

Jesus addresses the crowd: "A sower went out to sow." Everybody could relate to this scenario, because this is the way they lived. They were fishermen and farmers, herdsmen herding cattle, goats, and sheep. Some were traders and business people, but they either sowed seed themselves or saw others doing it season after season.

Now, when Jesus is speaking this to His disciples, He's showing them the timing of what's coming in the Kingdom. So He says, "The Kingdom of God is going to be like the sower sowing seed." Then He begins to define the function of this seed, focusing on where the seed is going to fall.

He says that the seed is going to fall on a kind of ground that's a pathway ground, a ground that is the religious world. There won't be much significance to the seed-taking root there because there's so much traffic. Broad is the way that leads to destruction but narrow is the way that leads to life; therefore, this path is the broadness of human habitation, thought, philosophy, ideology.

When the Word of God falls on this path, with the various things that happen there, people who have a purely rationalistic bent (like the Greek mind, or the Roman mind, or the Babylonian mind)—all of those minds that had been spawned throughout the centuries preceding the coming of Jesus—will not receive it. The Word is not going to take root because it has to be received by faith.

Then Jesus said there's another mindset amidst which the Word of God is going to be sown; it's going to fall amongst stony places and thorns. The thorns are like the cares of this world. Before the Word can actually grow in a person's heart, those cares can stifle its development. Then the Word is going to fall amongst stony ground, where it won't take root.

But then the Word of God falls on ground that produces three levels of produce—thirty-fold, sixty-fold, and a hundred-fold. This is interesting because we know that the Word of God is constant. It doesn't change, being the only thing that endures from generation to generation. But the same Word, the same seed, produces different levels of harvest—30, 60, 100. Why? Could it be because even though the Word of God might be sown in a particular place or a particular age, *we may fail to realize that God may have moved in His emphasis or preference in that particular place?*

Such failure means we stay in that place. We don't move with God's moving.

Live close to Him—and learn! My friend, will you move or stand still? Another way to ask the question is: Will you be one of the crowd or one of those disciples living close to the Lord? You see, it's important to notice in Matthew 13 that Jesus speaks parables to the multitudes but He gives *explanations* to the disciples. Jesus says to His disciples (not the multitude), "It is given unto you to know the mysteries of the kingdom of heaven, but to them it is not given" (13:11).

The English Word "mysteries" here is the Greek Word

mysterion. It means "a secret that is hidden." Once that secret is no longer hidden, it's revealed. Now, the apostle Paul says to the Ephesian church, "God reveals His mysteries to holy apostles and prophets" (3:3-5). So there are certain rankings of leadership in terms of exposure to the deeper things of God. Here Jesus says, in effect: "For those who don't have a higher calling in the things of God, I have to program their thinking by teaching them with stories."

I was raised in an era in which certain preachers, in order get somebody up to the altar, would tell us stories about a dog that was killed by a truck. People would start crying over a silly dog, and they would run to the altar because a truck ran down Rover. But did the preaching of the cross have a powerful emotional pull on the lives of the people? In some cases, no. Their hearts were stony to the Word, and filled with thorns. Or those folks were just immature in the faith. So the preacher had to tell some heart-rending stories about somebody getting hurt.

Mostly this reveals the immaturity of the listener. But Jesus says to those close to him: "You are not immature. You have an understanding of mysterion, the mysteries of the Kingdom. The multitudes are babies in thought. But not you. I have to feed those other folks with Similac, feed them with baby cereal," says Jesus. "I have to put purity in their mouths. I have to make a bottle for them to help them grow and develop."

But He says to the disciples, "That's not how I treat you. I reveal to you the meaty subjects of the Kingdom of God, not just the milk."

And that is how the Lord wants you to understand things, as well. His preference for a place and an age may change. Those with understanding will grasp it. They have lived close enough to Him to discern, wisely and well, all the motion that characterizes the Kingdom.

Seek God's preference—for THIS age. Dr. Peter Wagoner calls our age the era of "post-denominationalism"—where God is using independent visionaries as apostolic households to bring rank and to bring a release of the Kingdom.

Now here is where seeking God's favor and God's preference is crucial. I would like to suggest that God's favor and preference is not in the denomination. If the seed is sown in the denomination, it's only going to produce thirty-fold in this day and age. Same seed, same soil, but God's favor is not in that soil. But because the Word of God, Peter said, is incorruptible seed, it will produce a harvest in that soil nevertheless.

Now this is where the challenge comes to our church leaders. They can't be stuck in a religious mindset that looks to the past or stays tied to the status quo. If they are not seeking God's preference for this age, which may be a new way of working, then the Kingdom in motion leaves them behind. God's truth, of course, is unchanging down through the ages. But His methods may vary, age to age.

That's why the religious mindset and the Kingdom of God are two different things. It's why Nicodemus, in John 3, came to Jesus and said, "What must I do to inherit eternal life?" Jesus then begins to give him a Kingdom perspective. Nicodemus was a teacher, a ruler of the Jews, part of the theological training seminary for the next generation. Nicodemus, whose mindset was closed, came from a past denomination but also came to Jesus at night for a brighter future.

The night reveals that it was dark in the world of Israel and a new day was about to dawn in the Kingdom. And Jesus said, "Nicodemus, you have to be born again if you are going to enter the Kingdom of God. If you insist on confrontation of thought, idea versus ideal, you'll be religious the very next day. And you'll miss the great transition God is bringing to pass."

Stay constantly moving with God's Kingdom. What God did yesterday He may not do today. If he does it today, it's because of his grace. We're seeing, according to Acts, the restoration of all things, a restitution of things that were stolen and lost and misappropriated. It happened by human negligence and also by demonic persistence that pulled away from the human family.

What we have to see here, in our age, the church age of Ephesus, is that Ephesus had lost its first love. But "the first love" was not an affection. When the apostle writes that they lost their first love, he doesn't mean that they didn't love the Lord like they did in the beginning. That's ridiculous and even preposterous! Remember: These were the people who gave their lives, who died in lion's dens, who were burned with fire and sawn asunder by Nero. These people loved God with all their hearts and became the first martyrs. We today are weak and like milk toast in comparison to them. So when God says: "You've lost your first love," He wasn't referring to their affection for Him.

No, God was talking about the Ephesians' *position.* What was the first love of that church? The answer is given to us right here in Matthew 13: The first love was *understanding.* Jesus says here, "To you is given to understand the mysteries of the Kingdom." So instead of moving with God and what God was doing currently, they confronted the message, and they built churches.

The church-building concept was never in the mind of God for the Kingdom. "The Kingdom of God is among you," Jesus said. The Kingdom of God is in your heart. You take that Kingdom when you go home. You take the Kingdom when you go to your job. The Kingdom of God was never intended to be a participation of church players and spectators on a Sunday morning. The Kingdom of God was to go to your place and take over, to bring the influence of the Kingdom into every thing and every place you are!

Jesus was saying to the disciples, when the Kingdom of God is being preached, if you don't move with it, you will have thirty-fold instead of a hundred-fold.

It is moving, and you are invited to move with it.

The Raided Wheat: God's People Must Awaken

Now Jesus says that at night, while men slept, an enemy came and sowed tares in the wheat. It was a raiding operation carried out by the devil himself (vs. 39). But what shall we learn from it? I believe there are two critical points to see here—one about the enemy who stalks us and one about the success that thrills us.

The enemy will sow when you're asleep. Did you realize that you can have your eyes open while being fast asleep? You certainly don't need to be asleep to dream. But in a figurative sense, consider: I've seen men destroy their marriages because they were fast asleep, eyes open, and didn't know they were mistreating their wives (or wives mistreating their husbands). I've seen men of God lose members in their church because their eyes are open, but they're fast asleep in their vision, fast asleep in their philosophy, fast asleep to what God is doing today.

So Jesus says, "While men slept, the enemy came in and sowed tares." The tare is a counterfeit, and there are two ways you can tell what is wheat and what is tare. The first way is to look at the root. The tare grows around the wheat plant to choke out its life. Its root system is different from the root system of the wheat. Secondly, when it's harvest time, the truth is then manifest. What is truly of the Kingdom produces wheat; what is not of the Kingdom produces a gaudy flower. It has the appearance of feeding the nation, but in actual fact, it's not providing nourishment; it's actually a curse.

The message is clear: A time is coming when the church is going to be active in its state of so-called normality or development, but in actual fact, it's being put to sleep. And in this slumber, the enemy—the devil—is coming to sow false doctrine, to change our mindset and turn us away from a Kingdom perspective. He will turn us from the vibrant life of the Spirit and make us . . . religious.

The seeds of success will choke when you're proud. There is danger in being a leader in the church. We may begin with a visitation from God. We may be thrilled that God would speak to us in the middle of the night, maybe in the midst of a tough trial, and God will glow in our spirit and inspire us with a vision to change a nation. And then, when we gather people and we start getting money and become affluent and have Miss and Mister Uptown in church . . . then we build a cathedral.

And now because we're wearing expensive suits and we've got our Gucci, and our perfume, when it's time to worship God, we don't want to worship God as we used to. We don't want to jump and shout and run because, after all, we have graduated now. *Don't you know that I have a degree? My name is Mr. Fahrenheit and I'm married to Sister Centigrade.*

We've got a degree now, so we won't go back to the initial sense of visitation. In that moment of slumber, when we sleep and become inebriated and intoxicated by our own success, the enemy then comes in and sows the seed. And that seed is destructive, choking our spirit. It even chokes out the life of the Kingdom and produces a tradition of lackluster religion.

Religion stinks in the nostrils of God because it proclaims laws that have nothing to do with the Kingdom. It promotes a legalistic system that releases a curse. The Bible says in Jeremiah 17: "Cursed is the man that leans on the flesh, but blessed is the man who trusts in the Lord with all his heart."

Religion causes you to trust in your own ability, to trust in your flesh, and to trust in your money. You can sleep with your eyes open. Therefore Jesus said to this generation, "Listen! Don't fall asleep!"

He says to all of us today: *Awake! Move ahead with Me!*

For Group Discussion:

1. What is your definition of faith? How "healthy" is your faith these days?

2. Do you agree that faith can be "ruthless"? What does that mean to you?

3. When have you felt most in need of encouragement? Who helped you most?

4. What would it mean for you to "live closer" to Jesus? What first steps would you like to take?

5. How is the "religious mindset" such a subtle attack on the Kingdom? Where do you see this principle in action today?

6. Think about the times when you seem to be more asleep than awake to God's presence and work. How would you like the other group members to pray for you?

CHAPTER 7

Danger: Substitute Taste, Infected Kingdom

(Based on Matthew 13:31-36)

> *I will open my mouth in parables;*
> *I will utter things which have been kept*
> *secret from the foundation of the world.*
> —Matthew 13:35

At some point during their school days, most of our children will be taught about "The Danger Zone." It's a biological phenomenon that can occur in the family refrigerator any time "left-overs" are left over too long. It happens to foods that begin to decay and deteriorate over time. You open up that foil-wrapped package of once-delicious meatloaf and notice a dubious transformation: if it's fuzzy, if it's a bit green, if it smells a little funny . . . danger!

Jesus speaks of danger to the Kingdom. We must be careful to avoid this zone. In teaching about mustard and leaven Jesus tells us of influences that could prevent the glorious expansion of God's reign on earth. He warns of the potential for deterioration and decay.

Clearly, we must guard against any influence that could threaten the mighty work of God, the Kingdom in motion. Understanding the mustard and leaven will help us stay alert.

Mustard: A Pseudo-Flavor

Jesus says: "The kingdom of heaven is like unto a grain of mustard seed, which a man took, and sowed in his field: Which indeed is the least of all seeds: but when it is grown, it is the greatest among herbs, and becometh a tree, so that the birds of the air come and lodge in the branches thereof." The mustard seed is the least of the seeds in the herb family, but when this seed is grown, it has become something substantial.

One of the things I was taught about this parable in my early Bible school years was that Jesus was picturing the growth and expansion of the Kingdom. That is, even though a mustard seed is very small, sown in the ground, it will spring forth and bring forth great fruit.

But I see a more foreboding message here. I believe that Jesus is actually showing us the deterioration of the Kingdom in its progression. My reasoning goes like this: If you put mustard on meat, it takes away the true taste and value of that food and substitutes its own value. In other words, mustard offers what I call a "pseudo-taste." It takes the place of something pure and adds the impression of something else.

Why Hunger for a Substitute Taste? Jesus is saying that a time is coming when "mustard" is going to take away the taste of the Kingdom and substitute another taste in your mouth. If you eat a hot dog without condiments, you'll experience the true essence of what the maker of that particular food wants you to taste. But the minute you put ketchup or mustard or onions or anything else on that hot dog, then you're not tasting the meat. You're tasting a substitute taste. Similarly, the enemy is going to take away the true taste of the Kingdom and provide something else.

Are you prepared for this danger zone?

The first law of Biblical interpretation is that we must interpret the Scripture literally unless there's a valid reason to do otherwise (when we're dealing with poetic passages, for instance). The second law is to let Scripture interpret Scripture. So where the Bible calls something a branch at one point, in the future years it must also be understood as that. Now the Scripture here talks about this mustard tree growing up into a big experience, and Jesus says it grows so big that the birds of the air come and lodge in it.

He then begins to relate something we've never seen before, which is the deterioration of the Kingdom of God. In psychology there's a thing called the "crisis graph." It's a chronological charting of the crisis points of your life since you were a child. It shows the ups and downs of your experience. Perhaps during some years your life was going along normally, but suddenly you contracted a serious illness, or had a car accident, or suffered the loss of a bank account. The graph shows that you entered a downturn, an experiential abyss, as it were.

Down and down you went. You thought you had to have that man. Then suddenly you're at lunch with your friend, and in walks this man with someone else. Your heart is broken because the man you had dreams about marrying is sitting there with Suzy. You want to hurt him and Suzy at the same time! That is what this parable is like—*Jesus is now revealing a crisis coming to the church*.

You see, the devil is a liar. When Jesus died on the cross of Calvary, the Bible says the devil was going to bruise Jesus' foot, which was His mobility. But Jesus was going to bruise the devil's head, which is his governing entity. So Satan is, in a sense, analyzing this thing and says, "I've governed and controlled people before; I can do it again. I've just got to change their tastes."

How will you know when you're hungering for a substitute taste? I cannot say what it will be for you. Each person has his own particular vulnerabilities. But experience and observation shows that some of the enemy's most successful substitutes fall into well-worn categories. Have you ever hungered like this . . .

- Rather than pursuing a deepening fellowship with God in prayer, you form a relationship with a theology, a tradition, or even the image of your self as a holy person?
- Rather than praying *to* God, you spend your quiet time only thinking *about* God?
- Rather than encouraging your Christian brother in person, you reveal his "prayer needs" to another Christian (while not *really* gossiping)?
- Rather than coming to God in all your sin and weakness, you attempt to "clean up" first and present to God a substitute self that you hope will please him better?
- Rather than courageously standing for Kingdom values among your peers, you substitute a more "enlightened" viewpoint that is much more socially acceptable?

- Rather than viewing hard times as opportunities to grow stronger in faith, you seek various avenues of escape—shallow relationships, alcohol, pornography, religiosity, . . . (name your own favorite escape tactic here: _____)?

Surely you could identify more of the enemy's subtle substitute flavorings. But none of them can truly take the place of a deep and abiding relationship with God. None will prove a satisfying alternative. And none will help propel an individual, a church, or a nation into the flow of God's kingdom in motion in order to bring glory to His name. In fact, each is a cheap condiment that hides the true flavor of the Lord's greatness. Danger!

Taste and See that the Lord Is Good! The Bible says here (vs. 32) that the birds of the air were sitting on the trees, right in the house of God. This is not the first time it's happened; it was happening in Old Testament times too. Now think back and remember: What does Jesus say about the birds in the parable of the sower? He says that when the seed is sown on the pathway, the first to arrive on the scene are the birds. Who are the birds? The birds are the thief, and the thief comes not but to steal, to kill, and to destroy. So when the birds eat the seed in the first parable, it's the demonic word. Birds in the first parable describe the demonic word, and birds in the third parable describe what's sitting in the branches of the church.

The Kingdom of God is going to begin to deteriorate in its emphasis, so much so that the Kingdom taste will be taken away and a pseudo-taste will be put forth in the mouths of the hearers and the believers. In direct contradiction, you are called to taste and see that the Lord is good!

If you have mustard in your mouth, you'll never taste the goodness of God. It's the goodness of God that works repentance, and Jesus and John say: "Repent, for the Kingdom of God is at hand!" You'll never taste the goodness of God with mustard in your mouth. You'll never turn your thinking around to have your mind changed. And if your mind is never changed, Nicodemus, you'll never see or enter into the Kingdom of God.

Leaven: A Kingdom-Hatred

Now look at verse 33. This is even worse. "The kingdom of heaven is like unto leaven, which a woman took, and hid in three measures of meal, till the whole was leavened."

Now wheat is the Word of God. It is the element and degree of revelation. This woman, in light of Revelation 2, is Jezebel (that is, the spirit of Jezebel, or witchcraft). Again, I was taught in Bible school that this leaven was showing the expansion of the Kingdom. But leaven, in the Scripture, always speaks of sin. Therefore, it's consistent with any influence that tries to put down the Kingdom.

Close yourself to the Kingdom put-downs. Go back to the Old Testament with me for a moment. The second feast in Israel was the Feast of Unleavened Bread. The priest or leader had to go with a lamp to every corner of the house and take up the leaven. This was a sign of taking sin out of the house, because leaven (or yeast) always speaks of sin.

In the New Testament we find several kinds of leaven. For example, Jesus said, "Beware the leaven of the

Pharisees and the Sadducees." The leaven of the Pharisees is simply a hatred for the Kingdom, all wrapped up in hypocrisy. The leaven of the Sadducees is a neglect and rejection of the supernatural, since the Sadducees didn't believe in angels or the resurrection. So they despise the supernatural. Do you know anyone like that today? Run from that kind of Kingdom put-down.

Then there is the leaven of Herod: A hatred for a manifestation of the Messiah, because Herod killed all of the babies in Bethlehem in hopes of destroying the Messiah. The leaven of Herod means that whenever Jesus begins to manifest in a church—in music, in song, in thought, in worship, in idea, in the women, in the youth, in the children, in the men, in the preacher's wife, in the preacher somebody's going to stand up and criticize. In effect, they'll be trying to "kill" or char-acter-assassinate whoever is involved.

I've had people accuse me of being "too spiritual"! Has it happened to you, as well? Just because Jesus came into your heart in a greater way, has it threatened others and brought out a leaven of animosity? I say to you: pray a little more, worship a little harder, fast for a few more days, give a little bit more money, go the extra mile. It's alright if certain people close to you don't like it. Because now they can't tell the jokes they used to tell, can't announce to everybody what they did last Friday night and what drink they've been drinking. Because you are there, and you refuse to go that way. *Thus they want to kill the Messiah in you.*

Another leaven is Galatian leaven, namely, legal-ism. It brings the curse because legalism actually does away with the work of the cross, the finished work of Jesus Christ, and substitutes the works and actions of human beings. This is a doctrinal leaven that says your good works can earn favor with God and bring you to salvation. If your dress is long and the sleeves are long and your hair is right, and you don't wear makeup, you don't eat meat, you don't drink Coke—all of these things will get you saved. But of course the list of so-called good works is much longer than that, isn't it? It is, in fact, never-ending, depending on who is in charge. How much better to depend on the pure grace of God, mediated through the cross of Jesus!

So when Jesus says in Matthew 13:33, that a woman hid leaven "in three measures," he was actually talking about the extreme advance of the enemy's kingdom. If you're making bread, and you take a little bit of yeast and put it in that flour, you don't hear that yeast working. But if you let the dough sit overnight, you'll find that it is entirely under the influence of the yeast. So from birds in branches that don't possess the whole tree, to leaven that takes over the whole thing, Jesus is showing the deterioration of the Kingdom. Danger!

In the epistles, we find a wonderful apostolic restatement of the general principle Jesus expounds. I refer to Paul's words in Galatians 5:9—" A little leaven leaveneth the whole lump." He was warning those believers to flee a perversion, an infection, of the pure Gospel that would ruin their souls. One great Bible teacher[1] of the early twentieth-century wrote eloquently about this verse:

> It is only too true: the admission of a little false doctrine into the true is highly dangerous. One infected apple infects many others; the many sound ones never make the infected one sound. A little yeast alters the entire dough; the entire dough never turns

the yeast into dough. In our day especially, when so much is known about spores, ferments, and bacteriology, Paul's homely warning should be most effective. This proverb should be death to doctrinal indifference.

But many people still imagine that a little deviation from the truth of the Gospel will do no harm to them and to those who hear them. They even pride themselves on harboring at least some deviation and, while they want their food and their drink pure, cast their flings at the pure teachings.

What more can we say? Leaven always thrusts us into the doctrinal danger zone.

Open yourself to the Kingdom upswing. Now Jesus ends this teaching, sends the multitude away, and goes back to the house with His disciples (13:36). So we're going to shift gears here. Rather than focusing on the downturn in the crisis-graph of the Kingdom, we'll focus on the upswing.

Jesus goes back into the house and the disciples say to him, "Declare unto us the parable of the tares." So he explains the parable of the tares. But realize this: They've already understood, in essence, what it meant. I believe that *now Jesus was showing a separate sowing of tares.* Do you agree?

Let me explain by taking you back to the days of the Reformation in church history. In the early 1400s, a German Catholic priest named Martin Luther had a revelation of salvation. He saw clearly that salvation comes by faith and that the just shall live by faith, based on the writings of Habakkuk and Zechariah and Paul. He realized that when a person is saved, she is saved by believing the message of faith in this current season. She is saved by bringing her entire life to rely on that message. She is now living by faith alone, saved by God's grace alone. The Bible says, "For He that cometh to God must believe that He is, and that He is a rewarder of them that diligently seek Him." Because God looks for those who walk and live by faith.

So Martin Luther boldly declared that the just shall live by faith. He even nailed it on the cathedral door in Germany along with about a hundred other doctrinal reasons as to why he was leaving the Catholic church.

You see, Martin Luther's church had been slipping downward and finally hit rock bottom. Leaven had gone through all three measures of wheat. The whole church was under the influence of a diabolical attack by the enemy, an attack on the great truth of salvation by faith. But when Martin Luther got this revelation, he said we're moving forward with truth. So the circle of crisis began to swing upward.

On the upswing now in Matthew 13, Jesus begins to teach and interpret the sower and the tares, which should indicate to us that there was a second sowing of tares. Whenever revelation comes, your spirit opens to receive what God is going to give. When your spirit opens, it is at that point you are the most vulnerable. Why? Because you can see truth and a lie at the same time. And if you haven't been trained or conditioned to understand what is truth (because of your limited spiritual progress), you can actually fall for the lie. You enter a deadly danger zone.

And so, Jesus said there's going to be a second sowing of massive tares. I'm telling you, this generation is still reaping the results of those tares that were sown. Don't be a part of that sickly, infected harvest.

For Group Discussion:

1. When were you the hungriest in your life? When did you hunger the most for the things of God?

2. Have you ever eaten tainted food? How is this like receiving false doctrine in the church?

3. What specific substitutes for the Kingdom are most enticing to you, personally?

4. Which Kingdom substitutes are the most enticing to the church in our world today? In your community?

5. What does it mean to "kill the Messiah in someone"? How does it happen?

6. What, to you, is the main point being made with the story of Martin Luther?

7. What are your prayer requests today?

Notes: Chapter 7

1. R.C.H. Lenski, The Interpretation of St. Paul's Epistles to the Galatians, Ephesians, Philippians (Minneapolis, MN: Augsburg Publishing House, 1937), p. 267

CHAPTER 8

It's No Mystery: You've Got to Be Willing
(Based on Matthew 13:44-52)

Jesus saith unto them,
Have ye understood all these things?
—Matthew 13:51

We've been saying that the Kingdom moves forward in new ways. In verse 44 of chapter 13, we now have what most theologians call the last three parables. I take issue with that designation. I don't think these are parables in the fullest sense. They are actually three mysteries.

Why do I say that? Because the multitude wasn't there. Jesus had already sent them away and was now in the house talking to the twelve men He had given authority. They were the legitimate channel through which the Kingdom was going to be manifest. So He's talking to the boys in the house, and my point is this: Why should He want to tell them a parable if it's not given to them to be spoken to in parables (see 13:10-11)? To them it is given to understand *mysteries*.

Grab Hold of These Mysteries!
But here's where you come in. Are you, too, willing to understand the mysteries of the Kingdom and act

upon what you learn? These mysteries raise three critical questions for anyone who wants to move with the Kingdom that's in motion—

✳ *Treasure: Are you willing to find—but also lose your individuality?* Jesus is telling his disciples, "Here's a mystery. Don't go for the treasure, go for the field." A treasure was hid in a field which, when a man finds it, he goes and buys the field. The man is not interested in the treasure; he simply hides it. He then goes and sells everything he has. In other words, he loses his individuality. He sells everything that has identified him in the past; he puts all his reputation aside because he knows this field has a treasure in it.

✳ The point is clear: If I just go for the treasure, I don't get the field. But if I go for the field, I get the treasure. What we've done in the church today is try to build one ministry alone, our personal treasure. That's so unwise! If you're just building one church—New Life Covenant Church, or Bethlehem Pentecostal Church or Lutheran Specialist Church—then you're just going after treasure. But oh, Jesus says in chapter 13, when the sower went out to sow, that the field is the world. So what is He saying here? A man found a treasure in the world and, instead of just going for the treasure, he's going for the whole planet.

Jesus came for the world. He came to seek and to save that which was lost. Yet he didn't come just to save your soul; He came to put money in your pockets, to give you houses and lands. He doesn't want to just give you land, He wants to give you a country. He doesn't want to just give you a country, He wants to give you a continent. He's not interested in just giving you a continent, He

wants to give you the whole world! This is the Kingdom progressing, the Kingdom in motion. Rₒₒ 11: 15-
If the devil has the power to insert leaven and put the entire lump of dough under his influence—and the devil is the counterfeiter— then think of what God can do! If God comes and speaks a word into your life, He's greater than any leaven. He can bring an entire city under His influence.

We've taught for too long that the devil has such great power. But the devil isn't the CEO of the earth. He came to visit a long time ago, but God has given us the power and the anointing to take over. The Kingdom of God suffers violence, and the violent take it.

We've taken it back. And we want it all back—not just the power and the money, not just the treasure in the field. We want the whole field! Because Jesus said, "Occupy till I come." Therefore we're not just building a church, we're taking over more than that. We're going to own hospitals, schools and universities. We're going to own factories, banks, supermarkets, airline companies, medical insurance companies . . . taking over to influence every level of society with Kingdom values that bring peace and love and joy among all peoples.

Pearl: Are you willing to persist—but also be irritated? Look now at the next mystery. Jesus says, "Again, the kingdom of heaven is like unto a merchant man, seeking goodly pearls: Who, when he had found one pearl of great price, went and sold all that he had, and bought it."

Jesus once said, "Don't cast your pearls before swine." Now obviously, the pig doesn't understand value. You can take a pig to a beauty salon, give that pig a pedicure, a manicure, a back rub; you can perfume it, dress it with pink, purple, and yellow ribbons, and the minute it comes out of that salon, it's going straight to the mud. Because a pig doesn't understand anything that has value. So when Jesus says here that a man is looking for good pearls, He is speaking of the pursuit of revelation and of someone who knows value. A man is looking for good revelation in the Kingdom of God, and he's a persistent student.

How is a pearl formed? It begins with a little grain of sand that finds its way into an oyster's shell. It irritates this living organism, and the oyster begins to weave a smooth, protective coating around this sharp, scratching grain.

Being irritated, it begins to weave a thing of great price.

That's why, when a person is seeking goodly pearls in the Kingdom of God, there's always something that's an irritation to him or her. You become irritated with where you've been religiously. Somebody in your organization or in your church will say something that doesn't set right with you. For example, a preacher might get up one Sunday morning and say, "These women in this nation, who do they think they are? Women are just meant for the kitchen and the bedroom." As a woman, you know that's just not right. It irritates you, and you're not happy with being in that kind of oyster. You're looking for something else; you're looking for a goodly pearl."

I've been in places where, as a young preacher, I've been criticized for my philosophy, for what I believe God could do. One time we started supporting pastors in Zimbabwe—one in Chinhoyi, another in Mvurwi, one in Waterloo. But when my elders heard I was supporting these pastors, they came and criticized me. You see, it caused an irritation because I was seeking pearls of great price. I too was irritated, looking for God to do something special in my life. I wasn't satisfied with being in that oyster. So God began to weave around the irritation. He began to weave something that was special, and the more I stayed in God the more He showed Himself to me.

How is it with you? Are you willing to be a little irritated in order to experience more of God's goodness? Are you willing to be discontent with the way you are as a believer, willing to grow to the next level of maturity in Christ? Sometimes it means putting up with the most irritating of interruptions. Sometimes it means letting the irritations and tensions build in order to wait and see what God will make of them. Here is how one author describes the way it can happen:

> It is good to carry tension and not resolve it prematurely because, ultimately, that is what respect means. By not demanding that our tensions be resolved we let others be themselves, we let God be God, and gift be gift. . . . If only [we] would not panic and resolve the painful tensions within our lives too prematurely, but rather stay with them long enough, until those tensions are transformed and help give birth to what is most noble inside us—compassion, forgiveness, and love.[1]

You see, we have to begin to take a chance in the Kingdom and allow ourselves some tension. So many times we look at what we've invested in and we look at all we've worked for, and we weigh it and think it's heavy in terms of the little that could apparently result.

But we need to trust God when we're in Kingdom progression. Be ready to sell your reputation, sell your talent, sell whatever God has built in your life so far. Sell it all, put it all up for sale, and chase that one pearl. That pearl will buy more than you work for in a lifetime.

A rich young ruler came to Jesus and said, "What must I do to inherit eternal life?" He was looking at Jesus who is the pearl of great price. Jesus said, "Sell all of that and follow this pearl." If he had sold all that he had, he would have a pearl of great price, he would have received the pearl and even more. But what that man got was just his little bit of possession; he let the pearl of great price walk away.

Kingdom progression. When we see God doing something, we've got to be hungry for it and leave behind everything we've so carefully built. I see this especially in the American church where pastors build their kingdoms, and then God reveals truths to them that require following Him in a new direction. Will they leave what they've built so far and simply follow the Lord into the next Kingdom adventure prepared for them?

Dragnet: Are you willing to catch—but not get the credit? The third mystery is probably the most amazing. "Again, the Kingdom of heaven is like unto a net that was cast into the sea." Where do we find Jesus in the first parable? At the sea. At the first time, He doesn't cast a net; rather, He's sowing the seed. At the last "parable," He seems to say that where we start is where we end. We started sowing the seed but now we're getting the harvest. Jesus was telling the disciples that the ultimate goal is to fish in the sea of life: "Follow me, and I will make you fishers of men."

The last mystery is that a net is cast that gathers

every kind that, "when it was full, they drew to shore, and sat down." When you're fishing, you don't drag a net to shore, because you could tear the net. You lift the net, bring it onto the boat, and empty out the fish.

What Jesus is saying here is this: (1) There is no boat big enough to manage this catch; and (2) there is no boat that God wants to get the credit for this awesome catch. No human organization is going to get the credit for this catch. It's coming to the shore where multitudes sat—*and nobody owned the shore.*

Then Jesus sat down. In other words, there's going to be a release of anointed apostles and prophets who are going to be sitting in heavenly places in Christ Jesus. They'll be ruling and reigning with Him, gathering in what was lost, bringing in the choice catch. We're living in the most significant time. You have to understand that if you've been in the Kingdom net, you yourself are a choice catch.

God Isn't Sitting in One Place

Jesus would later say to Peter (in Matthew 17:27), "In order to pay your taxes, to meet a financial need, you're going to catch one fish that's got a gold coin that will meet all your financial needs." Imagine now, if you catch a net full of all kinds of fish that don't hold just one coin—but each has a bank in its mouth!

When the net was full, they sat down and sorted out the fish. The bad were cast away; the good was kept. And then Jesus asks: "Have you understood all these things?"

"Yes," they replied. They understood the progression of the Kingdom.

So my question is: Do you have an understanding of Kingdom progression? God is moving, he's not sitting

in one place. Are you ready to follow? Or are you too dis-
tracted, too content, too apathetic, or just too tired?
Don't be like the youth-camp counselor, whose story I
leave with you as my closing word:

> It had been an exhausting day; the guys in my cabin
> were asleep; and I was dead to the world. Then there
> came a dim awareness: Ants were crawling all over
> my body. I was so tired, and sleep felt so good, that
> I actually resisted rousing myself. I knew that if I
> were roused even a little bit, I would have to
> acknowledge that my sleeping bag had become an
> ant freeway. I didn't want to know the awful truth,
> so for at least several seconds I tried to fight it. At
> some deep level, I told myself that sleep was the
> reality and the ants were a dream.
> Apathy is sort of like sleeping through an ant attack.
> Waking up means I have to recognize that although
> foxes have safe places to hide, the Son of Man does
> not, and his followers do not either. This world is
> fundamentally opposed to me, and wants to attack
> me when I am least prepared for it. No wonder some
> of us would rather stay asleep.[2]

For Group Discussion:

1. Of the three mysteries, which speaks most powerfully to you? Why?

2. In the cause of the Kingdom, how willing are you to: Lose your individuality? Become irritated? Give up on receiving credit? If possible, share some personal examples!

3. What, specifically, will it mean for you to NOT resolve your tension in the days ahead? How difficult will this be for you?

4. Have you ever seemed to prefer "sleep" over attending to God's still, small voice? What happened?

5. What prayer requests are on your heart today?

Notes: Chapter 8

1. Ronald Rolheiser, The Holy Longing (New York: Doubleday, 1999).

2. Story told by Will Eisenhower, in Youthworker Journal, quoted in Craig Brian Larson, ed., Illustrations for Preaching and Teaching (Grand Rapids, MI: Baker Books, 1993), p. 8.

CHAPTER 9

A Brief Interlude—for a Look Back

(Based on Daniel 2:26-44, as background to Matthew 14 –17)

In the days of these kings shall the God of heaven set up a kingdom which shall never be destroyed and the Kingdom shall not be left to other people; but if that Kingdom shall break in pieces and consume all these kingdoms, it shall stand forever.

—Daniel 2:44

Gilbert K. Chesterton, the great English journalist of a century ago, once said: "Christianity has not been tried and found wanting; it has been found difficult and not tried."

It is difficult to be a Christian, isn't it? And it is challenging to advance with God as His Kingdom expands, moves, and progresses in constantly new and creative ways. Yet difficulty is no excuse to stand still. As the writer of Hebrews encourages us (12:1-4):

Wherefore seeing we also are compassed about with so great a cloud of witnesses, let us lay aside every weight, and the sin which doth so easily beset us, and let us run with patience the

> *race that is set before us, looking unto Jesus the author and finisher of our faith; who for the joy that was set before Him endured the cross, despising the shame, and is set down at the right hand of the throne of God.*
>
> *For consider Him that endured such contradiction of sinners against Himself, lest ye be wearied and faint in your minds. Ye have not yet resisted unto blood, striving against sin.*

No standing still! Jesus is our role model and forward-looking hero here. But looking back is sometimes allowed, especially when it helps us set the framework for a new work of the Spirit. In this chapter we will look back to the prophet Daniel, who gives us a powerful word concerning the Kingdom. His story is an excellent place to build a contextual foundation when we talk about the Kingdom in Motion. His courage amidst difficulty calls us, as well, to plow ahead through every adversity.

God's Man in Detention

You know Daniel's story of captivity. He and his people find themselves in a Babylonian culture in the sixth century, B.C. Now realize that when Babylon invaded a nation, they would leave the very weak in the conquered land but take the strong and healthy back to Babylon. They would leave the occupied territory with no government, no leadership, no vision; therefore, the area would revert to a political environment consisting merely of locally subsistent individuals. There would be no basic functioning economy, and no infrastructure. If you'll read 2 Kings 17, you'll observe how they took all the craftsmen, all the heads of state, and anyone who had any hint of leadership ability.

In other words, they left the broke, the busted, and disgusted in the land, where pandemonium reigned. Therefore, the people who were left had no sense of rulership, and no sense of direction. But Daniel did not remain behind. He was merely a teenager when he was carried away to captivity. In Babylon he was even given a new name: Belteshazzar.

Unknown to King Nebuchadnezzar, Daniel was a prophet—though even Daniel didn't discover this until he went into captivity. So, at the beginning of this captivity, which lasted for more than 70 years, God begins to reveal His plan. You see, the secrets, the mysteries, of God are given to those who are men and women of rank—kings, apostles, prophets, etc. And when we're talking about rank, it's important to know that rank is in direct correlation to, and also responsible for, government law, order, and structure in the Kingdom of God.

With Daniel, God is revealing what's coming in the future centuries. So God speaks to the highest-ranking individual upon the earth, which was King Nebuchadnezzar.

God's Message in a Dream

God speaks to Nebuchadnezzar in a dream and gives him a prophetic insight to what's coming in the future. But when God jumps out of the king's dream, God shuts his mind to it, but says to Nebuchadnezzar in his spirit, "You dreamed the dream, and you have to have the interpretation." So Nebuchadnezzar goes to all his fellows in the land—all the soothsayers, all the witchdoctors, all the opium men, all the warlocks and wizards—and says, "I'll pay you handsomely if you can tell me what I dreamt and give me the interpretation."

Of course, no one could read his mind unless God showed it to him! All these fellows, who are positioning themselves, for leadership, for money, for notoriety, can't give the dream because God shut it away from all of them. Because they are living in a world that's not a genuine world, it's a pseudo-world; a counterfeit world.

Then God reveals the king's dream/vision to Daniel. But it's more than just a vision being revealed. If God speaks to you in a vision, God's not just showing you what's coming in the future. If God takes the time to come and speak to you in a vision, He's telling you something about who you are.

The reason God was showing Daniel this vision is because Daniel now came to the realization that Nebuchadnezzar was the highest rank in the secular world, and Daniel was of equal rank to Nebuchadnezzar. But in fact, Daniel's rank surpassed that of Nebuchadnezzar because not only did he have the vision, he also received the interpretation.

So Nebuchadnezzar has a vision of a huge image. It has a head of gold. It has a chest and arms of silver. It has a belly and thighs of brass, shins of iron, feet and toes of iron and clay. Daniel says to Nebuchadnezzar, "This vision you have had is revealing the future of the Kingdom era, of all the rule of Gentiles." What you have is the decline in value of governmental systems, the decline of God's preference in terms of government.

The point for us today is this: *Christianity is now on the decline because we're failing to understand and exercise the power of the church.*

So Daniel begins to give his interpretations. As he

does, we will see something important to the unfolding of the kingdom in our day. You see, by looking at the progression of kinds of government, we see the preparation for a new form of rule on earth that is even now progressing and expanding in the twenty-first century. What are those kinds of government? Consider four that declined from God's original preference.

Gold: Rulership by person. This, of course, was God's original preference: rule by an all-wise, all-benevolent person. That is, rule by God himself. But if that is not possible, then rule by a completely God-dedicated man would be preferable. So Nebuchadnezzar is told by Daniel, "You, O king of the Babylonian system, are God's preference." It's God's golden order. That order is benevolent-dictatorial rulership. In other words, it's despotic or procratic, authoritarian rulership where you have one man on the top who makes all the decisions, wisely and equitably. Yes, surprisingly, that's what God's preference is. Jesus Christ is a dictator, whether you like it or not! When you submit yourself to the Lord Jesus Christ, you have no rights. No rights as a human being. All those rights are taken away from you.

But the difference is that Jesus Christ, in His dictatorial role as a despotic ruler, has a benevolent side to Him by which he gives you tremendous rights in terms of stewardship. You are a steward of your body, of your family, of your money, of the things you own, and of the community where you live. So, God's first golden order is autocratic rulership. The man on the top casting the vision for the Kingdom. Jesus said, "I am the vine, you are the branches. Without me, you can do nothing." He is the head, Corinthians tells us, of the body.

He is the head of the body, and without the head, we don't even have a body. You can do a heart transplant, but you can't do a brain transplant because the head is unique; it determines the entire function, composition, and competence of the whole body. So you can be kept alive on a machine, but if you're brain-dead, you're dead. So God's order here of headship is, firstly, the Babylonian system of one-person rule.

Silver: Rulership through law. The next best system is the governmental system of the Medes and the Persians, who came in and destroyed the city of Babylon. This was amazing when you consider the power and strength that was once Babylon. For example, the "Golden Mile" downtown was literally a street paved with gold. Babylon was the first economic system in the world to have what we call the Stock Exchange today, so this country was a very powerful order of government, of economy, of trade.

Nebuchadnezzar's palace had awe-inspiring "hanging gardens." Today's engineers are still trying to understand how Nebuchadnezzar could water these gardens through hydraulic systems connected to the Tigris and Euphrates Rivers. In science the Babylonians were advanced above all peoples of the day. It was the same in mathematics, philosophy, and all other areas of knowledge and skill.

And they were brought down by the Medo-Persians, according to God's plan.

So the Medes and the Persians came together, which is the second vision—a bear with two ribs in its mouth. The Bible says that the one rib was bigger than the other, which means that the one power was stronger than the other. But the rule of the Medes and the Persians was designed in such a way that there was a balance of power. And if a word, a rule, or a law was passed, it could not be changed.

That's why, when you read later on in Daniel that he was praying three times a day in defiance of the law, he was sealing his fate with the government. His enemies had told the king: "In the next thirty days, if anybody bows to any god other than you, let that man be thrown in the lion's den." They were setting up the king's main man, Daniel. So when the law was passed and the king sealed it, the law could not be changed. Daniel prayed, and had to go to the lion's den against the king's wishes. But the law was passed, and the law could not be changed.

So Daniel slept in the lion's den, but the king couldn't sleep. The next morning, when the king came to look and see if Daniel was alive, he found a bunch of sissy lions that had been turned into vegetarians overnight! Because God fixed it.

Once Daniel was taken out of the lion's den, the king could change the law because Daniel could go into the lion's den only once. The same lions that were to eat Daniel then ate his pursuers instead.

Brass: Rulership by the power of the intellect. Now comes the third best system of human government: rulership by the power of the intellect for utopian living.

Here Alexander the Great is the key player, at the head of the Greek Empire. This empire is shown in three aspects in these visions. The first is the belly and thighs of brass. The second is the leopard that moves at lightning speed, with the wings of a falcon. Then he's also shown as a he-goat, having one horn in the middle of his head that destroys a ram that has one horn bigger than the other.

What was Daniel seeing here? It was the progression of the governmental system of the earth. Daniel then shows that this he-goat comes with great speed and breaks the ram with two horns, which means that the Greek system led by Alexander destroyed the kingdom of the Medes and the Persians. Alexander's army moved with great speed and tremendous ferocity.

So, they conquer. The Greek system of government was based upon synthetic thinking. Under the philosophical influence of Socrates, "the Utopian endeavor" flourished. According to this concept, it was believed that, through its rulers' academic development and training, society could function with absolute perfection. After all, with rational thinking honed to a sharp edge, how could the human being fail to create the perfect city-state?

Wise thought would solve all problems; peace and prosperity would thrive among the Greeks.

Naturally, then, Greek politicians would be judged according to their academic performance. If they got to a certain age and they did not reach a certain level of performance in terms of their intellectual prowess, they would then be brought into a lower area of service. So there were apprentices, smiths (such as a blacksmith, goldsmith), craftsmen, builders, so on and so forth, right up the line, based upon intellect and artistic skill.

But can the intellect alone set up the perfect society? Certainly the apostle Paul had his doubts. This is why, when Paul went to the city of Athens to preach (in Acts

17), he began a rational debate with them. He saw all of their statues of gods and thinkers, and he said: "You Athenians, are too suspicious." Because he was dealing with men that were thinkers.

Now, just as an aside, let me warn against placing so much stock in the intellect alone. Today we're told that if we have an intellectually "enlightened" society, then, if a man is a murderer, you have to find out why he killed somebody. After all, if he did something so bad, there must be something good in him that was violated that caused him to be bad. If he's so bad, you've got to look for the good and do away with the bad. Rather than looking at the evil in him, in human nature, and punishing him for his wicked moral choices, instead we think we must give him counsel, put a television in his room, give him three square meals a day, and get the best psychologist to come and pick his brain. *Why did he rape these fifty women*, we wonder. We keep trying to tap his brain while refusing to look into his heart.

Yet, in terms of synthetic thinking, that's the way our world is today. It's why I'm very concerned about our young people leaving a church setting and going to universities to be exposed to this kind of thinking. If a young person is not strong in the Lord, this approach to human nature and society will shake the very foundation of his or her worldview.

Finally: Rulership through democracy, the rule of the people. We come now to the Roman order, rule through democracy. Even though there were Caesars, they were responsible to a consulate with senators who voted in this leader. The reason Julius was killed on the Ides of March, for example, was because he was being called by the people to take dictatorial rule.

The senators, such as Brutus and his counterparts, could not allow Caesar to be sole dictator in Rome. So they killed him in the senate, and they put his blood on their hands, and in so doing they collectively became responsible for his death. Marc Anthony was given permission by Cassius and Brutus in the famous play by Shakespeare where Marc Anthony addresses the masses of people. In his address, he constantly refers to these men being honorable men, yet they usurp authority by killing a man who had honorable aspirations. So we find democracy being released.

At the same time, there were other systems of government that the Roman system also released. We have the monarchy system, with kings who rule in kingdoms, princes who rule in principalities, and emperors who rule in empires. And all of these systems were part and parcel of the feet described in Daniel's vision. But the general consensus was that democracy—the rule of the people—was best.

God's Mandate for the Future: A New Kingdom

So this is what Daniel was seeing. But, my friends, Daniel sees something more. He sees a stone that comes out of the mountain. It arises without hands and smites the system of men. And this is why Daniel says that in the days of the world systems of government, there is coming another kingdom. This Kingdom shall never be destroyed. It is the Kingdom of God, led by the direction and auspices of the Lord Jesus himself.

So you can see: the Kingdom is new in its movement, each new morning. But it is not new in its conception. It has been the plan of God from before time. It was the plan of God even when God's people suffered captivity, time and time again. It is still God's plan today, a system that out-paces, out-performs, out-thinks, out-gives, out-loves, and out-governs every human kind of government ever devised or imagined. It is the rule of the one, all-powerful and all-loving King of the Universe in your heart and mind, in your family and mine, in your church, on your street, in your country. And finally, someday soon, it will be the rulership of this entire planet on that day when, without fail, at the name of Jesus . . .

> . . . *every knee [shall] bow, of things in heaven, and things in earth, and things under the earth; And that every tongue should confess that Jesus Christ is Lord, to the glory of God the Father.*
>
> —Philippians 2:10 11

For Group Discussion:

1. In your opinion, what is the best form of human government? Why?

2. Talk about a time when you have seen human government working well—and not so well.

3. How well would you fit into a benevolent dictatorship of Jesus right now? Is your heart already submitting to him daily?

4. What is your view of human nature? What is the "politically correct" view these days? (Refer to the author's comments about criminality that appear toward the end of the chapter.)

5. How would you like to pray for one another this week?

CHAPTER 10

Move Ahead, Even on the Water
(Based on Matthew 14)

Straightway Jesus constrained his disciples
to get into a ship, and to go before him unto the
other side, while he sent the multitudes away.
—Matthew 14:22

"Sloth is not to be confused with laziness," writes novelist Frederick Buechner[1]. "Slothful people . . . may be very busy. They are people who go through the motions, who fly on automatic pilot. Like somebody with a bad head cold, they have mostly lost their sense of taste and smell. They know something's wrong with them, but not wrong enough to do anything about. Other people come and go, but through glazed eyes they hardly notice them. They are letting things run their course. They are getting through their lives."

As the Kingdom Moves . . .

Just getting through life? That's not the Kingdom person! Rather, since the Kingdom is in motion, you and I need to move, too, in order to eventually become like Jesus himself. In light of Buechner's words, this clearly isn't movement without a purpose. We may see others in motion, but they may be slothful at heart. On the other hand, we may be calm and at peace, but hardly lazy. So you might be wondering: *What, specifically, are some of the movements we'll need to make along with the Kingdom?*

Consider three of them, which I'll unfold by asking some personally relevant questions you can answer in your own heart—

Have You Moved from Law to Grace? In Matthew 14 we find John the Baptist, who was a teacher of truth and repentance, saying to King Herod, "You cannot rule your kingdom and have your brother's wife." Therefore John was thrown in jail. And on Herod's birthday, his wife's daughter Salome was dancing seductively. Herod said, "You can have up to half the kingdom if you'll dance for me." So she danced and said, "I want John the Baptist's head."

Now John had to be beheaded. Even though it was a horrible way to go, the ultimate reason John had to be beheaded was because God was signifying through metaphors. Scripture says in Matthew 11 that John was the greatest of the prophets, even from the beginning of the prophetic age. So what happened was John lost his head, which showed that the headship and rulership of the previous system had to go because the headship of Jesus Christ in the Kingdom had to be reinstated. John didn't die of a heart attack or have his heart pierced out; no, his head had to go. That's why John was willing to give his head.

Now I want you to notice something about how his head was taken. It was taken by Herod and Herodias. They are the same spirits that you find with Ahab and Jezebel. They are the same spirits that you find with

Nimrod and Tamar. These spirits are constant, and they are current. They always go for headship. They always attack the leadership. They always go to take down what the Kingdom of God has been established to do. So when John died and lost his head, it was now a vacant headship for Jesus to move in and set up his Kingdom.

And what does Jesus do immediately thereafter? He performs a miracle filled with meaning for the kingdom (vss. 13-21):

> When Jesus heard of it, He departed thence by ship into a desert place apart: and when the people had heard thereof, they followed Him on foot out of the cities. And Jesus went forth, and saw a great multitude, and was moved with compassion toward them, and He healed their sick.
>
> And when it was evening, His disciples came to Him, saying, This is a desert place, and the time is now past; send the multitude away, that they may go into the villages, and buy themselves victuals.
>
> But Jesus said unto them, They need not depart; give ye them to eat. And they say unto Him, We have here but five loaves, and two fishes.
>
> He said, Bring them hither to Me. And He commanded the multitude to sit down on the grass, and took the five loaves, and the two fishes, and looking up to heaven, He blessed, and brake, and gave the loaves to His disciples, and the disciples to the multitude.
>
> And they did all eat, and were filled: and they took up of the fragments that remained twelve baskets full. And they that had eaten were about five thousand men, beside women and children.

When John's headship is taken off, and Jesus' headship is put in place, we now have in Kingdom progression what I call the Multiplication of the Kingdom, because of the feeding of five thousand. When Jesus puts the anointing on five loaves of bread, we must understand that five is the number of grace. *He had now done away with the law and brought grace.*

This is no small thing. It is a movement in the Kingdom that we too must take up or we will never even get close to the Lord at all. To live by the law is to be completely outside the Kingdom. But to recognize our inability to experience fellowship with God by our own means is the most blessed movement of all. We give up on our works and trust Christ's work on the cross. We give up on our righteousness and cling to Christ's righteousness alone, for He fulfilled all of the law perfectly on our behalf.

We even give up on the idea that there was something good within us that God saw and which therefore caused Him to extend His grace. We give up, as well, on the idea that there was something potential within us, which God saw could happen in the future, and therefore He saved us. No, He saved us when we were sinners. He saved us only because we qualified in one way: we were totally lost. So, I ask: have you moved from law to grace? And if so, are you able to extend grace to others, especially when they don't deserve it?

I am reminded of the World War II concentration-camp survivor, Corrie Ten Boom. In her book *The Hiding Place* she tells the story of when she was engaged to be married to a young man she deeply loved. But this man disappointed her greatly. He broke off the engagement without warning and married Corrie's best friend instead. Corrie was confounded and became terribly isolated and alone. Until her father told her:

> Corrie, do you know what hurts so very much? It's love. Love is the strongest force in the world, and when it is blocked that means pain.
> There are two things we can do when that happens. We can kill the love so that it stops hurting. But then of course part of us dies, too. Or, Corrie, we can ask God to open up another route for that love to travel.[2]

Corrie did open her heart to the movements of God's love. She was able to live by grace thereafter and extend it to others. In fact, there came a day when, years after she had endured the horrors of the holocaust, she met one of her former jailers—and extended God's grace even to him.

Have You Moved from Self-Rule to Kingdom-Rule? Let's look more closely at this miracle of feeding. In Matthew 14:15, we read that it was evening, in a desert place. We are, in this generation, living in the evening time of the existence of man. It's evening time now when Jesus says to his disciples, "We've got to feed these people." The disciples say, "Why don't you just send them home?"

But sending people to their own homes, to their old system of order and government is not going to work. They have to be fed by the hand of the Kingdom. Ultimately, all of us have to give up on self-rule, our belief in our own self-sufficiency. So Jesus then says, "Tell these people to sit down because this young fellow brings five loaves and two fish." Here we see what can happen when you have Kingdom rule. The systems of man can't feed them in their houses and sustain them on a three-day journey, but Jesus could provide for the multitude in less than five minutes in one afternoon. Because when you have order, when you have Kingdom government, structure, and rulership, you can do more in a nation than if you have a hundred denominations going their own separate ways.

That's why it's important to persist and pursue unity among church leaders in your hometown. I can recall a few weeks ago when we had a prayer meeting in Harare, Zimbabwe, at an international conference center, and something wonderful was released there. We were responsible as the Kingdom of God in our city and our nation, responsible for the peace that prevailed and the calm that prevailed during the Zimbabwe elections.

Jesus said to his disciples, "I'm going to show you what you can do when, as apostolic headships, you put your minds together on one cause." Here in Matthew we have thousands of people needing to be fed. Jesus says, "You guys can't feed them, but I'm going to take five loaves—what can't feed a little boy. But when twelve apostles in the Kingdom in Motion, in Kingdom government, come together, you can feed people in any desert place, in the middle of a drought."

Have You Moved from Your Side to the Other Side?
So understand what Jesus is saying in chapter 14: "If you will trust in me, I'm going to show you Kingdom alternatives. You can send these people home, or you can feed them." The option or the preference is: you can feed them.

Now, there's another option he's giving them here. He

then says to them in that same chapter, "Go to the other side." Because at some stage or another, as the Kingdom of God, as a church, as a family, as a woman, as a man, as an entity of a company, you're going to have to go to the other side to explore what's happening there. *You don't have to do what everybody else is doing; there is a Kingdom alternative.*

They get into the boat because their fathers did it, and that's the way everybody else does it; get into the boat and go to the other side. Jesus then goes to the prayer room. They should have asked Him, "What is the alternative to get to the other side?" He had just shown them the Kingdom in Motion, always as a Kingdom alternative. The Kingdom alternative was, feed the people before you send them home, instead of sending them home to go and find food. Here's another alternative: Go to the other side. They just didn't ask; they didn't get the lesson the first time. So they got in the boat.

Have you considered alternatives to the way you are living your daily life? To the way you are conducting your church life? For example, it's 10:00 A.M., you start church, you sing three fast songs, two slow songs—maybe you'll bow and maybe you won't, and somebody might give a prophecy—then the choir will sing, then there will be a word on giving, then everybody must stand and give their tithe, then the preacher will stand and preach. In the middle of his message, the organ will play, and he'll sing while he preaches, and everybody will shout and you'll then go home and talk about what a great service you had.

It was a great service, but it hasn't changed the nation, hasn't changed the community! Our fathers are still drunk, our people are still broke, our girls are still pregnant, and we're still suffering—*because we haven't exercised a Kingdom alternative*. No, we just get in the boat and do what we've done every Sunday. Isn't this a terrible form of sloth?

But Jesus says: "Go to the other side." They should have asked Him, "What's the alternative?" He showed them what the alternative was. They were rowing to go on the other side . . . and here comes Jesus, walking on the water.

As I Am, You Can Be

I want to show you something. Jesus was teaching them, "As I am, you can be." In chapter 10, Jesus taught His disciples this: "You can never be greater than your master, but you can be as He is. What they call the master, they will call you."

So He's showing them here that if He's walking on water, then they too can walk on the water. That's why Peter said, "Lord, if that's You, tell me to come." The Lord said, "Why don't you come?"

Peter got out of the boat and the others were saying, "Stay in here, Peter! Don't rock the boat. Our fathers have never done this. Moses rolled the sea apart. Joshua rolled the Jordan apart. The least you can do is stay in the boat!"

Peter must have recognized that there's always a Kingdom alternative. Therefore he said, "You tell me to come out, Jesus."

If we're going to understand the function of the Kingdom, there's always an alternative. We don't have to do the same things the denominational structures have always done, what our forefathers have always done.

The alternative is simply to do it the way God wants it done. It's "not by might, nor by power, but by my Spirit, saith the LORD of hosts" (Zechariah 4:6). Ask Him how He wants it done.

Look how He fed Israel. He fed them with manna from heaven. He took dust and made chicken. He didn't dig a pool hole, He commanded water from a rock! The same God will fight your battles; the same God will open doors for you, because there is always a Kingdom alternative.

The governments of this world tell you there are certain things you can and cannot do.

Don't listen. Don't stand still.

Move ahead.

For Group Discussion:

1. Do you agree with Frederick Buechner's definition of sloth? How would you say it in your own words?

2. Where have you seen sloth, or laziness, in your life? In your church?

3. What would it mean for you, personally, to "get out of the boat," like Peter did?

4. What Kingdom alternatives are opening for you these days?

5. What Kingdom alternatives are opening for your church? (Suggestion: Spend time brainstorming some of the possibilities.)

6. How can others pray for you as you seek to move ahead with the Kingdom?

Notes: Chapter 10

1. Frederick Buechner, Wishful Thinking: A Seeker's ABC (San Francisco: HarperSanFrancisco, 1993), pp. 109-110.

2. Corrie Ten Boom, The Hiding Place (Washington Depot, CT: Chosen Books, 1971), p. 47.

CHAPTER 11

Doors Will Open, Eyes Will See

(Based on Matthew 16:13-19 and 17:1-21)

He saith unto them,
But whom say ye that I am?

—Matthew 16:15

Caesarea Philippi was once a small town now enlarged and beautified by Phillip the Tetrarch, one of Herod's sons. Clearly this son was proud of his work, since he named the city in honor of both Caesar and himself.

From ancient times the place was filled with pagan temples. One of its most notable deities was the Greek god named Pan. Even today, visitors to the city (now named Banias) can explore a grotto shrine dedicated to Pan and the nymph Echo. The shrine was built into the side of a cliff, over the source-springs of the Jordan River, and adjacent to a great cavity that opens up in the earth. During ancient times, the people in the area tried to measure the depth of that hole, but its bottom could never be reached. Therefore, it became known as the place where Pan would go down to the underworld, Hades—the "Gates of Hell."

Yet the city's fresh-water pools, fertile environment, and snow-capped mountain vistas made it one of the most pleasant resorts in Palestine during Bible times. In addition, the city boasted a great, white-marble castle, built to honor the godhead of Caesar. It sat there gleaming in the sun, high up on a mountaintop.

This is truly an amazing place for the kinds of things Jesus will be doing there, as we read in Matthew 16 and 17. After all, at Caesarea Philippi the people enthusiastically entertained the gods of sexual perversion. Pan, the half-goat, half-man was, in effect, the region's tribute to homosexuality. In fact, the place became such a seething cauldron of illicitness that when Jesus and his friends came into Caesarea Philippi, they literally entered a land of orgies.

So Jesus now comes to the region, and He's standing there looking at these gates of hell. He turns to His disciples in the middle of the street, with tremendous presence amidst the spirit of Jezebel. And He raises questions.

Let Us Answer His QUESTIONS

Here in Matthew 16:13-19, Jesus calls us to "open" the Kingdom in all places, by truly knowing Him, by using the authority He gives, and by opening every place wherever we are. We begin by responding, personally, to the riveting questions he ask us—

Question #1: Will You See Me As I Am? Here at Caesarea Philippi, amidst all the false deity-worship and degradation, Jesus wants a declaration of Kingdom reality. "Whom do men say that I am?" He asks. That word "men" refers not just to flesh and blood; He's talking about the systems of the world. What do the systems of this world say I am?

His disciples answer: "Some say that thou art John the Baptist; some, Elias; and others, Jeremias, or one of the prophets."

Remember that Jesus had already said to them, "To you it is not given to hear parables, but you have been given to understand the mysteries," so these men must come to understand the mysteries of the Kingdom of God. Walking with Jesus, they could see He was a mystery himself because they could never quite figure Him out. Today He's walking on water; tomorrow He's sitting in a certain place. This day He's a baby in Bethlehem, tomorrow He's resurrected and walking in a certain way that the boys on the road to Emmaus couldn't recognize him. They couldn't figure him out, because Jesus was a mystery. And just by being with Him, understanding Him meant understanding the mystery.

So He asks further, "But who do *you* say I am?"

Peter then gets up and says, "Thou art the Christ."

Let's analyze that for a moment. That word "Christ" is the translation of the biblical Greek word *Christos*, meaning "anointed"—the anointed flesh, the anointed entity that God has brought on the earth. The synonymous Hebrew word is Messias, or Messiah. The anointing of God upon the earth. "Thou art the Christ, the son of the living God."

Jesus marveled and said, "Flesh and blood…" referring, in other words, to the systems of man. "The thinking order of humanity hasn't exposed this level of revelation to you. But my father, who takes His hand off the secrets, has opened this to you. Because now that you are learning to understand Kingdom perspectives, Kingdom alternatives, and the Kingdom in Motion, you shall have the keys to the Kingdom of heaven."

How are you answering this question? Is Jesus truly the anointed one for you? Is this clear in the way you order your life—from your daily priorities to your all-encompassing lifetime goals and purposes? If so, then Jesus has keys ready for you.

Question #2: Will You Be Ready to Use My Keys? Yet Jesus wasn't giving Peter keys, as you'll see if you read verse 19 properly. He wasn't saying, "Here are the keys to the Kingdom." He was saying, "I will give you the keys." In other words, it's for a future date. If I say to you, "You're going to New York City, to go to my apartment in Manhattan." And I tell you, "I'm going to give you the keys to my apartment." What I'm telling you is this: I don't have the keys here with me, but when you get to 51st Street in Manhattan, somebody's going to be there to make sure that when you get to my door, you have the appropriate key to open that apartment.

What Jesus was saying here to these fellows was, "Peter, when you get to certain barriers or certain doors to go through in the Kingdom, then you will have the keys to get in." Peter wasn't just given keys.

Jesus then says, in essence, "What you declare with your mouth to be legal will be legal. What you declare to be illegal will be illegal." In other words, you are going to get to certain places where that word "legal" is referring to government rule and order. He says, "You're going to get to certain places in the Kingdom of God where you will make irrevocable statements concerning the status of the earth, the status of humanity. And once you say

'Devil, that's illegal, get out!' then the devil has to move."

You can walk into a place where, like the gates of hell, the things done there shall not prevail, even where the devil seems to have taken over completely. I don't care if it's Pan, the homosexual God; I don't care if it's Herod and his system. Peter, if you walk through the gates of hell right now with the knowledge you have concerning the Christ and the Kingdom, you can walk through the gates of hell and confront this entire system in Caesarea Philippi and declare it illegal! It will cease to be.

Jesus wasn't just speaking words to them. He was speaking the most basic truths of heaven, to them and to us. It all comes about through opening ourselves to Jesus, walking close to Him each moment, and staying in prayer. Pastor Jim Cymbala, who wrote a book called *Fresh Wind, Fresh Fire*, says it like this:

> Satan's main strategy with God's people has always been to whisper, "Don't call, don't ask, don't depend on God to do great things. You'll get along fine if you just rely on your own cleverness and energy." The truth of the matter is that the devil is not terribly frightened of our human efforts and credentials. But he knows his kingdom will be damaged when we lift up our hearts to God.[1]

Question #3: Will You Let Me Work—Anywhere?
There's no system in the world that's too hard for a man or a woman of the Kingdom. Your city is not too hard. Harare is not too hard. Johannesburg is not too hard. Kingston is not too hard. Dallas is not too hard.

London is not too hard. Baghdad is not too hard. In the city of Kandahar, in Taliban territory, that's not too hard.

If you go with the eyes of the Kingdom and stand in the gates of hell and declare, "Thus saith the Lord, thy Kingdom come, thy will be done," the systems of the world have to bow down.

But on the most personal level, will your own ego bow down? It is quite easy to be saved: you simply accept God's gracious gift. But to live as a saved one is difficult, requiring a constant, daily letting go. Yet it is eternally worthwhile.

Give up your self, and you will find your real self. Lose your life and you will save it. Submit to death, death of your ambitions and favorite wishes every day, and death of your whole body in the end: submit with every fiber of your being, and you will find eternal life.

Keep back nothing. Nothing that you have not given away will ever be really yours. Nothing in you that has not died will ever be raised from the dead. Look for yourself, and you will find in the long run only hatred, loneliness, despair, rage, ruin, and decay. But look for Christ and you will find Him, and with Him everything else thrown in.

Let Us Look at His GREATNESS

Not only are there questions for Jesus' disciples (which includes you and me) to answer, but there are things for them to see, as well. So we now move on to Matthew 17:1-21 in order to view an amazing appearance. The Bible says Jesus goes up into a high mountain with Peter, James, and John and that there Jesus is "transfigured." In other words, in a physical sense, the light in His being shows forth.

I want to tell you that we are about to see something similarly profound. We are about to see an awakening—not of churchianity—but of the Kingdom of God. And what shall we fix our eyes upon? Look—

Look at Our Great King: Showing Forth His Being. As I've said previously, blood in a human being's veins is congealed light. When Adam and Eve were in the Garden of Eden, they didn't have blood flowing through their veins, it was light. How do we know that? Well, we look at when Jesus was glorified, when He stepped in the room and said to Thomas, "Feel me, because a spirit hath not flesh and bone, as you see me have." All Jesus' blood had been drained on the cross. He still had veins, but what was flowing through His veins? It was light, or glory.

So what happens now on the Mount of Transfiguration? Jesus' blood—blood that comes from His father, for the Bible says, "What was conceived in Mary was of the Holy Ghost"—begins to glow before these three fellows. Appearing with Him is Moses and Elijah.

Moses was the one who saw from the beginning and recorded it, all the way to the establishing of theocracy through the Jewish system. Elijah was sent to protect it as a front to deal with Jezebel. If you'll read 1 Kings 16, you'll see that Elijah was released because Ahab, the king of Israel, married Jezebel, a Sidonian princess. Jezebel was literally a spirit medium, in that her body was given over for a demonic prince to possess. The demon that came into the woman Jezebel was the demonic prince Jezebel itself.

Look at Our Great Kingdom: Coming to Earth. The demonic world functions in this way: There is Lucifer on the top, three generals under him: Jezebel,

Death and Hell, and Antichrist. All of these three generals have a system that serve under them, which also
include the whole hierarchical system of the demonic
world.

So Ahab married Jezebel and brought this witch,
this demon, into the house of God by covenant. Now
that the demon was in Israel, God had to raise up a
governmental headship by the name of Elijah. That's
why when John the Baptist came Jesus said, "John has
come in the spirit of Elijah." To do what? To challenge
Herod and Herodias, a governmental system trying to
overrule the world.

Thus Elijah was a governmental headship, and
Moses was a governmental headship. So here, they're
talking to Jesus not just about Calvary but about the
government of God coming to the earth. Peter, James,
and John are witnessing this thing.

Government is rulership on another level. When
Jesus was transfigured, an aspect of endorsement was
released for his government that was about to be
established. That's why, from chapters 17-21 of
Matthew, the role and function of Jesus changes totally and completely. He now starts handing out His
authority to each of the apostles and disciples because
they are about to rule and reign with Him in heavenly
places.

Look at Our Great Challenge: Afflicted Institutions.
Closing with this, in Matthew 17, the Scripture reveals
the first thing that happens when Jesus comes down
from the mountain. He now faces a demon in a boy
that His apostles could not cast out. But Jesus comes
and casts out that devil.

Our greatest challenge is casting out the demonic spirits in institutions, the ones that have been, in a sense, "possessed" for so many years. The only way we're going to do it, the only alternative is to do as Jesus said, "This kind comes out, but by fasting and prayer."

Let Us Establish His Government

We know that Jesus dies in Jerusalem. When He dies, all the Jews are shouting, "Kill him! His blood be on us and upon our children! We have no king but Caesar!" That same bunch, fifty days later, are in the streets repenting of their sins. How did that happen? Well, the devil had come to Jerusalem and tried to establish his rule. A few days later, the government of God came upon the anointing of the apostles, and they took over. What they saw Jesus do by casting the devil out of that boy, they did in Jerusalem—they cast the devil out, and the Kingdom of God came rushing in, so much so that the priests even began to repent for what they had done.

The answer in the church today is the establishment of the government of God. When you see the Kingdom in Motion, it's literally where apostolic rulers and headships throughout the world are coming together and releasing the power of the Kingdom. It comes through a contemporary Kingdom word; through the demonstration of the Kingdom by miracles, signs, and wonders; through God lifting up nations as a demonstration of His power; and also by God lifting up minority groups of people who have been constantly oppressed.

Are your doors open to this Kingdom? Are your eyes ready to see?

Chapter 12

Go Beyond the Limits, Part 1
(Based on Matthew 18:1-14)

*Verily I say unto you, Except ye be converted,
and become as little children, ye shall not enter
into the kingdom of heaven.*

—Matthew 18:3

There's a story about the vain Russian empress Elizabeth Petrovna (1709-62), daughter of Peter the Great, that goes like this: It seems she was absolutely in love with the color pink. She was so jealous of this tint that she issued a decree making it a capital crime for any other woman in her empire to wear a pink garment—visible or concealed. The empress prided herself on being an opponent of capital punishment, but any woman caught in violation of the pink law was liable to torture or deportation to Siberia—or both.

The Tsarina's selfish and self-centered attitudes continue to astound historians today. She was apparently totally self-focused, especially smitten with her own beauty. It's said that her wardrobe contained over 15,000 dresses, over 5,000 pairs of shoes, and a clothing bill so large that certain French suppliers eventually cut off her credit. Yet Elizabeth would spend countless hours dressing, undressing, and redressing in order to admire her own beauty.

Naturally, her attitudes and actions hindered and limited the proper rule of her kingdom. And that is my point for bringing her to you as an example; she is the exact opposite of what a Kingdom person should be: "Whosoever therefore shall humble himself as this little child, the same is greatest in the kingdom of heaven."

In this chapter and the next, we're going to look at four hindrances to the Kingdom in Motion. In focusing on this theme, I hope it will become clear to you that certain attitudes and actions truly do hold back the expansion of God's rule on earth. In order to stay in motion with the Kingdom, avoid these hindrances at all costs—

Hindrance #1: "Don't Need a Thing!" (A Solo Attitude)

In Matthew 18:1, the disciples came to Jesus with an interesting question: "Who is greatest in the kingdom of heaven?" Now, the answer they were expecting is not the answer Jesus gave them.

> *"Jesus called a little child unto him, and set him in the midst of them, and said, Verily I say unto you, Except ye be converted, and become as little children, ye shall not enter into the kingdom of heaven. Whosoever therefore shall humble himself as this little child, the same is greatest in the kingdom of heaven. And whoso shall receive one such little child in my name receiveth me.*
> *But whoso shall offend one of these little ones which believe in me, it were better for him that a millstone were hanged about his neck, and that he were drowned in the depth of the sea."*
> —Matthew 18:2-6

What is all of this in terms of a Kingdom? What Jesus was saying here is that if you are going to be the greatest in the Kingdom, you have to be as a little child—not be *childish* in your attitudes and actions; rather, be *childlike*. I spoke in a previous chapter about immaturity, how we have babies in Christ, how babies drink milk and can't chew on the meat of the Word. So it would seem here that Jesus was contradicting himself regarding spiritual development. After all, isn't it the fact that being a grownup gives you the right now to bear fruit of your own?

But let's look more closely, since what he's saying here is an amazing truth. Jesus was saying that a child, in his or her infancy, is *totally and absolutely dependent* upon its parents. A child cannot live without receiving everything from its parents. So the whole child's persona, demeanor, attitude as a whole is totally and irrevocably dependent. And this is the way we must be in the Kingdom of God.

You cannot come into the Kingdom of God thinking you know everything—wanting the best seat, wanting to be on top of everything, or even wanting to reserve certain colors for your own use, ala the strange Tsarina! When you come into the Kingdom of God, you have to be like a child whose parents say, "Over the weekend, we're staying at the beach."

That is an announcement over which the child has no choice. He's going to the beach and, furthermore, he receives these instructions: "We're going to have a picnic there; we're having dinner at a nice restaurant in the evening, and the next day we're going swimming. So you will take swimming trunks, a nice pair of clothes, and a pair of jeans and a T-shirt."

The child can't argue with that because the parents

are telling him where they're going and what they're going to do when they get there. The child has no say in this. He is not paying for the fuel in the car or the food along the way. He must simply get into the "kingdom vehicle" and go where the "kingdom" is going.

Jesus was saying here that if you are going to see the Kingdom of God progress in your life, you'll have to be like that child. You have to stop being an adult when it comes to an attitude of defiant independence—"I don't need anybody. I don't need that preacher, I don't need that church, I don't need that revelation; I'm going to build my own thing here."

No, humble like a child, you remember that God is about to make a move at any minute; you have no choice. When it's time, you've got to pick up your bed and walk, if God is saying, "Walk."

Simply put: *self-centeredness is death to the Kingdom.* I am reminded of a statement made by one of President Theodore Roosevelt's children: "Father always had to be the center of attention. When he went to a wedding, he wanted to be the bride. When he went to a funeral, he was sorry that he couldn't be the corpse."

Is this your attitude these days? Must the spotlight always be shining on you, your work, and your needs? If so, you may very well end up in a state of spiritual deadness.

Our children don't tell us what to cook in our home. If there's food on the table, they have to eat what's on the table. When we're training them, we say: "Make your bed. Clean your closets. Pick up your shoes." They have to do what we tell them to do because it's part of their training. It's also a way that we parents can show our deepest love and concern for them. We want them to grow up strong and healthy and competent. Would we want it to be any different between us and our heavenly Father?

Hindrance #2: "Feudin' and Fightin' " (Church Conflict)

Now Jesus goes straight into what happens if I am an independent thinker and can't seem to function with a childlike attitude: "Offenses will come."

But will we get beyond those offenses? Or will we, instead, hold grudges, fume, fight, and hinder the Kingdom with our screaming voices and kicking feet?

It's amazing how adults can so quickly revert from *childlike* attitudes (which Jesus called for) to *childish* behavior (which Jesus would condemn). I once saw some kids fighting with their neighbor's kids—one family's child hit the other family's child. The parents heard about the fight and, years later, the parents are still sore about it. They're still not talking to each other! But the kids are friends; they were friends ten minutes after their little squabble. Because children have a way; when it's over, it's over. They move on together.

Since offenses will come, though, Jesus has more to say along these lines: " Wherefore if thy hand or thy foot offend thee, cut them off, and cast them from thee: it is better for thee to enter into life halt or maimed, rather than having two hands or two feet to be cast into everlasting fire" (18:8). Jesus isn't telling us to literally cut off our hands and feet, of course. He's offering an analogy here of the Kingdom in terms of feet— meaning to walk in a certain place: "The steps of a good man are ordered of the Lord."

So if your feet are not active by going into the Kingdom, then Jesus would rather you go nowhere at all (rather than hinder progress in the Kingdom). If your hands are not building in the Kingdom, it would be better that you don't build anything than to build something that was totally antagonistic to the Kingdom structure.

Jesus then begins to talk about a shepherd who goes and looks for one sheep that was lost. There were 99 in the fold, but one was lost. There are a number of things in this parable that we need to understand. If we look at the number 100, where we have a reaping of 30, 60, 100 (in the parable of the sower that Jesus tells in Matthew 13), a hundred is the maximum by which God is going to move in a powerful way in reaping when the Kingdom is in Motion. He says here that if you are functioning in the Kingdom of God, and you are not reaping at a hundred-fold blessing, somebody—or one aspect of the Kingdom—is not in place.

Don't go ahead until you have restored what is missing. That is, you can't say, "Forget about *that* city" and move on. If God has brought into the camp of the Kingdom-leaders certain men, and if you know that a certain leader or pastor or headship has to be a part of that group—Jesus was saying *don't try to move ahead into greener pastures without bringing that one individual or that one ministry into this place.*

You'll be moving maimed! Literally and powerfully God is saying there are certain components in a city, or certain components in a nation, in terms of ministries, in terms of leaders, in terms of churches, that are absolutely necessary.

Therefore, we have to get along if we're to carry out God's will in all places. God doesn't put all of his revelation, all knowledge, all wisdom, in one ministry. He doesn't put it all in one church. God doesn't gift one church with everything. If pastors feel that way, they are being foolish. God never invests all of his gifts in one group alone. That's why Jacob had twelve sons and not just one. Each of his boys had a different gifting and anointing. God gave Ruben one gift, Simeon another gift, Levi one gift, Judah another. Each of these men received a different gift and, together as twelve tribes, they became a great nation.

Jesus is saying to us today: "You need each other. You can't be 99% together, and leave one behind, and think you're going to win the city and get the sheepfold to a place of power. If you're going to take a city, you have to have 100% of the Kingdom of God functioning there. If it's not, leave your gift at the altar, go and find the missing component before you move ahead."

The church in Zimbabwe, the church in London, the church in New York, as individual ministries, all have powerful groups. But those groups are not infecting an entire nation. They're not bringing change to an entire nation. The only way that's going to happen is when all of the sheepfolds come together, when the shepherds agree to come to the one well and drink at the same time from the blessing of God.

Sadly, offenses come. Hindrances happen. But aren't you tired of it? I'm so tired of selfish thinking. I'm so tired of inhibited thinking and how it limits the progress of the Kingdom of God!

For Discussion

1. When have you felt as if you really didn't need a thing from anyone else? What things did you learn during that time?

2. Have you ever seen the damage that church conflict causes? (Talk about it constructively, if you can; don't name names).

3. In your opinion, how can a church avoid conflict? How can conflicts best be resolved in the church (refer to Matthew 18:15-27)?

4. In what ways is your church working toward unity today?

5. How would you like to pray for your church and other congregations in your area?

CHAPTER 13

Go Beyond the Limits, Part 2
(Based on Matthew 18:15—19:30)

Then came Peter to Him, and said, Lord, how oft shall my brother sin against me, and I forgive him? till seven times? Jesus saith unto him, I say not unto thee, Until seven times: but, Until seventy times seven.
—Matthew 18:21-22

In general, it's very easy for us human beings to become offended. And it's just as easy to become offended in the Kingdom of God. Here's an example: I was preaching the other day, and I made a statement that I was quickly going to explain: "White people are strange."

If I had stopped at that point, I could have offended a certain gentleman from Australia who was sitting in the first row. But I began to qualify what I said by talking about "the horror movies syndrome"—how, if there's a squeaky door in one of those movies, you always find the white person going back to inspect it in order to see what's behind that door...

But we black people will be running away!

Yes, I was just trying to be funny. But somebody

may just hear that first part and get absolutely, extremely offended. *This preacher is a racist*, they'll think.

It's so easy to be offended. And since offenses will come, Jesus speaks of our problem with unforgiveness, a serious hindrance to the Kingdom in Motion.

Hindrance #3: "Forgive and forget? No Way!" (Unforgiveness)

Jesus tells a parable about a servant who owed his master millions of dollars. The servant couldn't pay, and his master said, "I'm canceling that debt." So the servant walks out of the house and finds somebody that owes him ten bucks. He says to this guy, "I'm taking you to jail, I'm putting you in prison, because you haven't paid me ten dollars."

Then the master says, "I've just canceled a million dollars of debt for him, and he's putting his own debtor in jail for ten dollars? How in the world can this be?" He says, "Take this man, put all the debt he owes on him again. All that debt that the other man owes, put it on him also. Throw him in jail and don't let him out. He cannot be a part of the Kingdom anymore."

I have seen in the body of Christ all over the world, where pastors don't talk to one another. Because so-and-so said that, so-and-so did this, and they release into the body of Christ—and into their own church and their own spirit—the spirit of unforgiveness. Jesus indicates here to His disciples that if you want the Kingdom of God to progress in your life and in your ministry, you cannot afford unforgiveness. Unforgiveness is the only sin that makes you accountable for everything you have ever done in the past.

The hindrance of unforgiveness happens in this way. Let's say you've been involved with drugs before the

Lord delivered you. Now you're delivered, and you're serving God in the Kingdom. You may even become a preacher.

Suddenly somebody does something to you. For example, a group of people leaves your church (and maybe they're the "money people" in your church), and they go over to this other person's church. So now you're angry and upset because your money people are now sitting in that church. And this other pastor welcomes them and doesn't talk to you about resolving the issue.

So now you become filled with unforgiveness. What you have actually done is to disqualify yourself from progressing in the Kingdom! Because you're stating that the people that are the money people are your source of finance, not the Lord. You are opening the door for all of what you used to be to come flowing back to you. This is why people face lust and sin and treachery in their lives, because of unforgiveness. The minute you have unforgiveness in your life, everything you ever did in the past comes back to you. When that nature comes back to you, it slows down the progress of the Kingdom.

"I must forgive." Jesus made this point very clear when Peter asked, "How many times must I forgive somebody that trespasses against me?"

Jesus said, "For each offense, seventy times seven." In other words, if somebody offends you, you must forgive them seventy times for that one offense, times seven. So if you say something derogatory to me, that hurts me as a man, as my culture, as my race, I have to forgive you not just one time but 490 times. I have to forgive you for one thing that you do 490 times. And if you do it ten times, I have to forgive you 4,900 times.

The reason is that if I don't forgive, the Kingdom does not progress.

Let me give you the classic example of the Kingdom in progress: "Father, forgive them, for they know not what they do." The last thing Jesus prayed was, "I cannot have unforgiveness in my heart for these people who are murdering me and killing me and accusing me of something that I have not done." The very moment He prayed that prayer of forgiveness, He opened the door for the Kingdom of God to move from a Judaism-position to a Gentile Kingdom position—self-forgiveness.

One of our greatest challenges in working with pastors is helping leaders to forgive one another. I was in one of the most powerful corporate cities in the world for "faith generals." Yet that city as a whole is probably one of the most destitute cities, spiritually. There's practically no revival there. The reason for it? You've got the great faith generals who don't talk to each other. They don't have meals with each other, they don't share coffee with each other, they don't invite each other to one another's conferences.

It's not that they have unforgiveness in their hearts; it's just a lack of unity and genuine coming together. That should not be. If those men would ever come together in solidarity, it would open the door to the Kingdom of heaven, and God would show up in a powerful way.

We live in the city of Harare, Zimbabwe. Our responsibility in the city we live in is to do everything in our power to get pastors together and keep them together. When pastors make irresponsible statements concerning another race, we have to call them to accountability and tell them, "You cannot say things in the newspaper or on the radio that are irresponsible, things that would hurt another church and hurt another man. That kind of thing produced unforgiveness, and the Kingdom of God cannot and will not progress."

This why Stephen, when he was being stoned, looked up to heaven and said, "Father, forgive these men; they don't have a clue of what they're doing." After Stephen was stoned, the Gospel spread all over the known region, because one man forgave and opened the Kingdom door. But be assured: unforgiveness will hinder the progress of the Kingdom.

Dissing the Deals (Not Respecting the Covenants)

In Matthew 19, Jesus begins talking about marriage and divorce. Yet, in my opinion, He's not just dealing with the marital relationship. He does, but His words apply to the progression of the Kingdom as well. You see, marriage is a covenant. When a man and a woman enter into the covenant of marriage, as did Adam and Eve, we realize that what God has put together, no one should put asunder, regardless of the type of "putting together."

In Israel, if a man was not happy with his wife for whatever reason, he could just write her a note and say, "I divorce you." Finished, over and done! No paying back, it's over and done. But a woman could not write a letter to divorce her husband. Thus Jesus was saying that once you come into the Kingdom, you'll find that it's built on relationships that are just and right, covenantal and accountable.

A great hindrance to the Kingdom moving forward occurs when people don't observe their relational covenants. In other words, if you don't understand that the Kingdom language is a language of covenant, then the Kingdom of God will never progress. Sooner or later you're going to have to make levels of covenant agreements and allegiances with people.

In relationships, there are three things that have to be in place for the Kingdom to move: (1) an allegiance. Allegiance means you will join forces with somebody for the purpose of winning battles. (2) Allegiances come into agreements. There are certain people that you come into agreement with where you now pledge a certain level of loyalty. (3) Then there is a level of covenant. Covenant is where flesh is cut and blood is shed, and you are now willing to put aside your individual DNA and bring together corporate DNA.

To illustrate, I will say that I am in covenant with men in my life, but that covenant isn't as deep and intimate as the covenant I have with my children and then with ChiChi. ChiChi and I have the deepest and greatest covenant of intimacy, for she is the only human being that should see me naked outside my doctor. In other words, there are certain things that are private and only available to certain levels of covenant. You don't take off your clothes to everybody; you don't reveal your secrets to everybody. You don't tell everybody your problems. There are levels of covenant.

What I find in the body of Christ is a lack of covenantal commitment and relationship. For example, people don't stay friends for very long. That's why the body of Christ is so messed up, because we have preachers who don't have any friends. We have preachers who are not accountable to anybody for their marriage, for their ministry, for their money, or for their church's money. They'll sin today, and next week they'll come back to the same church and the foolish members are still sitting there listening to this man who has broken the relationship with them long ago.

If I have a relationship to somebody else, and I am accountable to somebody else; if I behave like a fool and begin to be sinful, then that person has to call me to account and bring me into order.

Jesus was not just referring to marriage here. When I got married and put this ring on my finger, it meant that no other woman in the world could enter into ChiChi's space; we are in covenant. If they come into ChiChi's space, I have broken the progress of covenant in our lives. The same is true in the covenant of relationships in the Kingdom of God.

Now Jesus reinforces all of this when a rich man comes to him and says, basically: "I want to serve you. I want to give everything I have to you."

Jesus says, "Sell all you have and follow me."

The selling of all you have is what Jesus literally did. The Bible says in 2 Corinthians 5:21 that "He hath made Him to be sin for us, who knew no sin; that we might be made the righteousness of God in Him." Second Corinthians 8:9 says, " For ye know the grace of our Lord Jesus Christ, that, though He was rich, yet for your sakes he became poor, that ye through His poverty might be rich." Jesus was willing to give up everything to open the door for the Kingdom. What He was doing for this rich young man was saying, "You have to be willing to give up your past life."

When I got married twenty years ago, I gave up my life for another life. I used to live as Tudor Bismark, the single man. I had my own money, my own bank account, my own things. But when I got married, I gave all of that up because now someone else had given up her old life to form a new life with me. We closed the old to open the new.

Jesus was saying to this rich man: If you're going into the covenant relationship to be with me, you have to be willing to give up everything of the past. That's why churches and ministries that do not put aside their personal agendas for the corporate agenda never get to taste the fullness of the Kingdom. Your agenda must not supercede the Kingdom agenda.

In the city of Buenos Aires, Argentina, a number of incredible things have happened because church leaders there agreed to put aside their differences, to respect and honor each other, and to pray with and for each other. What they have struggled to do as separate churches during fifty years, this handful of men did in less than seven years. Churches today in Argentina have three to six million in membership. I know one church that now holds services seven (7) times every day, virtually around the clock. The reason these things have happened, I believe, is because men came into covenant with one another. They were no longer limiting and hindering the Kingdom. They put aside self-centeredness, conflict, unforgiveness, and lack of accountability. They came together, and God opened heaven over their heads.

That's the Kingdom in progress.

For Group Discussion:

1. Why is unforgiveness so dangerous to the church? What is the solution?

2. How would you define a "covenant relationship"? What are some of its characteristics?

3. What forms of accountability do you have in your life these days? What about your church leaders? (Do they need to be asked about this?)

4. Who do you need to forgive at this time in your life? (Don't necessarily answer aloud; just allow for a period of silence so group members can prayerfully consider their responses.)

5. Talk about what forms of forgiveness and/or accountability might be needed among you.
Then . . . pray for one another!

COVENANT PARTNER INFORMATION

Dear Friend,

Thank you for taking the time to take a closer look at Jabula – New Life Ministries. While our ministry is taking us to the United States, Canada, the United Kingdom, and other nations around the world, we are endeavoring to answer the call of God in our homeland of Africa. God has given us a specific mandate to EMPOWER the people of Africa, by providing for them in a number of areas. Truly God is blessing in unprecedented ways, but at the same time, the needs of people are growing, the costs to bring this needed help are escalating, and our economy at home is in absolute demise. We must depend on the support of our friends in the United States and Europe to empower us to continue these efforts.

I want to personally ask you to prayerfully consider becoming a Covenant Partner with us on a financial level. As you covenant together with us for this Kingdom mandate, we believe that you become a part of God's blessing as well. Thank you in advance for your role in helping answer the call of God. May God richly bless you, and open the windows of heaven over you life!

Sincerely,

Bishop Tudor Bismark

Below is a basic outline of what God has called us to accomplish for His glory.

Jabula Medical Program

- Medical Mobile Clinic
- Ambulances for Emergency Transfers
- Seeing between 1,000 to 1,500 Weekly
- A wide range of diseases (HIV, Cholera, TB, Skin issues, etc.)
- Medical/Hygiene packets

Orphan Relief and Assistance

- One in four Zimbabweans is an orphan
- Currently providing for over 100 children
- Provide housing (build orphanage facilities)
- Provide food, clothing, and medical care
- Provide educational assistance

Education Program
(Jabula Foundation)

- Currently providing education assistance to over 2,500 children
- Provide teachers' salaries
- Build schools and classrooms
- Provide books and supplies
- Commitment through college degree

Widows/Elderly Care

- Caring for over 3,000 widows and elderly
- Provide housing (build living facilities)
- Provide food, clothing, and medical care

Ministry/Pastors Support

- Provide covering to over 1,000 pastors
- Operate Bible schools in several locations
- Provide monthly financial support for over 200 pastors
- Provide regional conference to train and empower

For more information or to
send a donation, please visit
our website:

www.jabula.org

or contact us:

United States
Jabula-New Life Ministries
445 E. FM 1382, Suite 3-371
Cedar Hill, Texas 75104

(800) 671-0844
E-Mail :
info@jabula.org

Jabula Bookstore

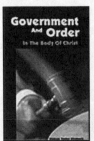

Government and Order
Bishop Tudor Bismark
Audio Cassette-5 cassettes
$30.00 +S&H

In the last days, God said he would rebuild the Tabernacle of David. This is the re-establishing of the Government of God. In this series you will learn principles like; Basic Church Government, Kingdom Government, Restoring Order and more.

Breaking Curses
Bishop Tudor Bismark
Audio Cassette-4 cassettes
$25.00 +S&H

Are you continually encumbered with sickness, financial bondage, temptation, or poor relationships? Do you feel like you will never break through? Learn how to be free from issues you thought you had to live with! Audio Set - 4 cassettes

The Anointing of a Thousand Times More

Bishop Tudor Bismark
Book
$10.00 +S&H

Will open your eyes to the power of God's anointing, and show you practical ways to prepare for this impartation. God is awakening the church to be life changers, city changers, and world changers!

JABULA BOOKSTORE

The Anointing of an Apostolic House
Bishop Tudor Bismark
Audio Cassette-5 cassettes
$30.00 +S&H

God is establishing and raising up Apostolic houses which will bring order and government back to His Kingdom. In this series, learn some of the key characteristics of Apostolic Houses.

The Ministry of Intercessory Prayer
Bishop Tudor Bismark
Audio Cassette-2 cassettes
$12.00 +S&H

We are living in the day of the greatest prayer movement that has ever been in the history of mankind. The number of Christians praying today far exceeds the total number of believers that have prayed in preceding centuries and millennia.

All these items **and more** may be ordered at our website:

www.jabula.org

or through mail or phone at:

Jabula-New Life Ministries
445 E. FM 1382, Suite 3-371
Cedar Hill, Texas 75104, USA

(800) 671-0844 • E-Mail :info@jabula.org